Jenny Dalenoord Drawings

Government Publishing Office, The Hague, 3rd revised edition, 1983
ISBN 90 12 04247 X

Frank E. Huggett

the dutch today

The Netherlands is a country of great contrasts

and contradictions. It is a little scrap of waterlogged land which is less than half the size of Scotland or the American state of South Carolina; yet it has been responsible for creating some of the biggest multinational companies outside the United States – Philips, Royal Dutch/Shell and Unilever. It is known as a respectable conformist country; but the night life in Amsterdam leaves little to the imagination. It is known everywhere as a Protestant country; but the majority of church-goers are Roman Catholic. It is one of the most domestic and home-loving countries in the world; but most people are content to live in rented flats or houses. It is a nation which fought a protracted eighty-year war against Spain in the sixteenth and seventeenth centuries to gain its independence as a republic; but in 1813, the Dutch people, reversing the usual pattern of history, chose to live under a monarchy which they have devoutly supported ever since. The unexpected has always happened in the Netherlands, but never more so than in the last twenty years.

The American author, Washington Irving, once wrote a story

about Rip van Winkle, a Dutch immigrant in New York, who had a drink with the crew of a mysterious Dutch ship, the *Hendrick Hudson*. He went to sleep for twenty years. When he woke up, his daughter was married, his village had been rebuilt, and the United States had gained its independence. A modern Rip van Winkle who went to sleep shortly after the end of the Second World War would be equally astonished by the changes that have taken place in the Netherlands in the last two or three decades.
Scarcely any other country in western Europe has made so many fundamental alterations in its attitudes, its economy, its way of life, with such outstanding success and, relatively, so little friction and violence. It is one of the great post-war success stories.
The Netherlands emerged from the last war with Rotterdam, its biggest port, and parts of many other towns in ruins; nearly a hundred thousand houses destroyed; and almost a quarter of a million acres of land under water. Many people were starving and eating rotten potatoes or even tulip bulbs just to keep alive. In 1949 it lost an empire, the Dutch East Indies (now Indonesia), a

vast archipelago of three thousand islands, many of them fantastically fertile, which had provided rich supplies of rubber, tea, fibre, tin, oil and spices. Four years later, the sea broke through the dikes in the south-west of the Netherlands, flooding more than half a million acres of land and killing nearly two thousand people.

The outlook seemed bleak. An empire lost; war-time wounds. In many ways the Dutch seemed unprepared by circumstance, if not by nature, to cope with these disasters. The basis of their pre-war life, a large overseas empire, trade and agriculture, was in ruins. There was little natural wealth – no minerals, not a great deal of coal. There was very little heavy industry. And mentally many of the people seemed to be unprepared for change. Society was rigid and old fashioned. Wives could not open a bank account without their husband's permission. Men and women up to thirty years of age had to obtain their parents' permission before they could marry. There were some parts of the country, strict Calvinist strongholds, where life seemed scarcely to have changed since the Middle Ages.

Now all that has changed. Rotterdam has been rebuilt and greatly expanded. It was one of the first cities in post-war Europe to be constructed in the modern style, with a central pedestrian-only shopping precinct – the *Lijnbaan* – containing wide, flower-fringed pavements and adjacent cafés, shops and blocks of flats. In the south-west, one of the most ambitious flood prevention schemes ever undertaken – the Delta project – has reached its final stage. The economy has been transformed with about one-third of the working population now employed in industry.

And many of the Protestants, once separated into segregated sects, have become increasingly interested in unity with each other and in the growing ecumenical movement. Most of the rigid barriers which kept the people apart in the pre-war years have been painlessly torn down.

In the past, some very uncomplimentary remarks have been

made about the Dutch. Most of the English phrases relating to them, such as Dutch courage, Dutch treat, Dutch uncle, were coined in the middle of the seventeenth century when the English waged a ceaseless propaganda campaign against the Dutch as a prelude to the first two Anglo-Dutch wars of 1652-4 and 1665-7. The English aim was to destroy the Dutch supremacy in world trade and shipping. Although they succeeded partially, the Dutch have the distinction of being the last nation to invade England, when ships commanded by their brilliant admiral, Michiel de Ruyter, sailed up the Medway to Rochester and Chatham and burnt or captured a number of English warships, including the English flagship, the *Royal Charles,* which was taken back in triumph to the Netherlands.

The tendency for 'Dutch' to be used in a pejorative way has persisted into modern times. Most foreigners wrongly believe that Dutch elm disease started in the Netherlands. They are usually astonished to be told that it started elsewhere and that the name is intended to be an international scientific tribute to the excellence of Dutch research into the disease. At the Forestry Research Station in Wageningen two new varieties of elm have been developed, the Commelin and the Groeneveld, which it is hoped may be fully resistant to the disease. The Dutch intend to lose as few of their own trees as possible. In 1970, Amsterdam became the first city in the world to use a new technique of infra-red

J. DALENOORD

Scheveningen

photography from the air to spot invalids among its 240,000 trees.
On the photographs healthy trees show up as bright red; lighter or
darker shades can spell danger.

This new technique has enabled the city's tree doctors to reach
hundreds of their patients before they succumb to a fatal disease.
It is like having an annual medical check-up for each tree. In spite
of this, many foreigners continue to believe that the Dutch were in
some way responsible for elm disease. Faced with such ambiguous
compliments about their own achievements, the Dutch find that
their rather quiet, restrained sense of humour helps. As in
England, it can often be directed against themselves. The Dutch
don't shrug their shoulders much, but mentally they are always
doing so. They need their sense of humour. It is one of the ways

Rotterdam Port

in which they manage to preserve their sense of tolerance and 'let it be' towards other people in what is one of the most densely populated countries in the world.

Over fourteen million people live in the Netherlands.

The average density of population in 1981 was 419 per km² and in the western part of the country it is very much higher. About five million people live in the *Randstad,* or ring town, which is about the same size as Greater London. Forty-five miles long and forty miles across at its widest point, this huge, horseshoe-shaped conurbation contains most of the major cities and towns, including Dordrecht, Rotterdam, Delft, The Hague, Leiden, Haarlem,

J. DALENOORD

Amsterdam, Hilversum and Utrecht. What makes it unique is that each city still basically does its own thing and that there are wide open spaces of pastureland between most of the cities. Rotterdam, the biggest port in the world, handles nearly two hundred million tons of goods a year. Amsterdam, the capital, is the financial and cultural centre and The Hague is the seat of government, with the Houses of Parliament, the foreign embassies, and the International Court of Justice. (Dutch people used to say that you made your money in Rotterdam, spent it in Amsterdam, and talked about it in The Hague.) Utrecht is the main communications centre and Hilversum is the radio and television city.

The former monarch, Queen Juliana, chose to live some twenty-five miles away from the capital in the unpretentious Soestdijk Palace; but her daughter, Beatrix, the present queen, has reverted to the mainstream tradition by setting up her residence in The Hague. She lives in the Huis ten Bosch, the House in the Woods, which was built as a summer residence for the Orange family in the seventeenth century and converted into a small, modest palace in the following century.

The closed end of the *Randstad* rests on the North Sea coast and the two arms open out to embrace dairy-farming meadows, so that no inhabitant is very far away from either the country or the sea. From The Hague, for example, it takes only fifteen minutes for a flat-rate-fare tram to clank and sway through woodlands and parks to the seaside resort of Scheveningen, with its bracing air, which was one of the favourite summer resorts of the European aristocracy by the end of the nineteenth century. It is now being restored to some of its former glory as an all-season seaside resort, with indoor swimming pools, shops and saunas and a concert hall and a casino in the recently renovated Kurhaus. But if you want to see Scheveningen as it was before either the aristocrats or the modern tourists took over, you have to go back to The Hague! There, in the house which was owned by the seascape painter, H. W. Mesdag, is a fascinating painting which gives a panoramic view of Scheveningen when it was a small fishing village in 1880. You have to walk along a darkened corridor in the small museum and climb a flight of spiral stairs to reach a gallery, where you are completely surrounded by a vast circular painting of the beach, the fishing boats, the bathing house, the small cottages and the canal leading to The Hague. The circular form and the clever use of perspective, the concealed lighting, and the simulated sand dunes stretching out between the viewer and the painting, which are littered with coils of rope, anchors and clogs, give a remarkable impression of being there, in person, a century ago. With a circumference of 394 feet and a height of 46 feet, it is one of the largest paintings in the world, yet it took Mesdag only four months to complete it, with the aid of his wife and two other painters of The Hague school, Breitner and De Bock. The Panorama Mesdag should be on every tourist list.

Dutch towns are connected by a highly-efficient rail network. The trains leave and arrive as punctually as the canal barges did in the seventeenth century when they provided the Netherlands with the first scheduled passenger transport system in the world.

There is also a comprehensive road system of motorways and throughways. These roads could be built dead straight in this flat countryside, but they are deliberately kinked just to keep drivers awake. Bridges are more common than tunnels, which are difficult and expensive to build in land below sea level. Before the war, there was only one tunnel in the whole country, the Maas tunnel in Rotterdam; but now there are an increasing number and two underground railways, one in Rotterdam and the other in Amsterdam to the new satellite town of Bijlmermeer, eleven miles away. In Amsterdam, the tunnels were forced into the earth by compressed air, while the soil below was sucked out – a remarkable engineering feat.

Driving through the historic centres of some cities can be anything but easy. The narrow bridges over canals, the numerous pedestrian precincts and the one-way streets, can make it seem like a journey through a maze, with drivers setting out east to reach some destination in the north. The Dutch accept these difficulties with a reasonable degree of tolerance, though sometimes the hooting of horns, the throbbing engines of heavy lorries, and the high-pitched drone of mopeds, or *brommers* (buzz-bikes) as the Dutch call them, can sound like an experimental session for a modern industrial symphony. The city centres, however, do not seem so crowded as, say, Oxford Street in London or Fifth Avenue in New York. This is partly because all the residents in the conurbation do not have to flock into the same city centre; each city has its

11

J. DALENOORD

own shops, entertainments and attractions, which are near enough to be used by people who live in the other cities. Some of the cities are more crowded than others, particularly Amsterdam which is one of the most popular tourist centres in Europe. But even in the summer, when Amsterdam can be very crowded, you can usually find a quiet place for yourself along by the tree-shaded canals. The concentric design, the comparative smallness make the capital an ideal city for the stroller or the wanderer.

This applies even more strongly to The Hague, with its central lake right by the Houses of Parliament, its pavement cafés and its winding arcades, full of floral decorations. A walk round the Plein, where some of the Ministries are situated, particularly on a Monday morning when the shops are closed, really does convince you that The Hague is the largest village in Europe, as the inhabitants, half-proudly, half-ironically, proclaim.

If you have to live in a conurbation at all, this is probably the best way to do it. Instead of one sprawling metropolis, or a multitude of scattered urban centres, there are a few big cities surrounded by a number of smaller towns and villages in the green belt. The belt has been threatened in places, particularly around The Hague, but it is still generally intact. Dutch planning has been praised by many foreigners. As one British planning expert, Peter Hall, has said: 'There seems little doubt that for most of the rapidly-growing world cities of the present time, the Dutch solution is the right model.'

Many of the Dutch, however, would not agree. They find their cities cramped, their lives confined, by the smallness of their country. People in the *Randstad* often have an urge to flee. It is easy for them to do so. They take a train or drive to nearby Germany, Belgium or France. In the summer they go further south in search of the sun or north to Ireland, Scotland or the Scandinavian countries for the peaceful isolation that is more difficult for them to find at home.

The feeling of constriction is understandable. After all, when you are living in a small city like Dordrecht or Leiden, with a population of around one hundred thousand, it is a little difficult to accept that you are really living in a conurbation containing five million people. In Dutch cities, small-town manners, customs and curiosity tend to be retained. There is no escape into anonymity as

13

there is in London or New York.

Dutch houses have large windows not only to let the sunlight in, but also to allow people to see out better. The Dutch like to know what's going on in the outside world. Many of the older houses still have a *spionnetje* (spy mirror) bracketed to the window frame outside to make it easier to see into the street. Equally, the Dutch do not resent other people looking into their homes, and rarely draw their curtains at night, though in the last few years more people have started doing so. Urban life has less exclusiveness than it has elsewhere. Heavy curtains do not cut you off from other people; but you become the target for many eyes. People still look or even sometimes stare at you in the street. (Don't worry; there's usually nothing wrong!) In conversation, the Dutch have not lost the habit of honestly looking other people straight in the eye. They have developed a civilised code of social manners and behaviour in which the unexpected is not expected to happen, though because of the Dutchman's inherent individuality, it sometimes does. The ideal is the golden mean. They are polite, but not effusive; not assertive, but insistent on their rights. They neither push nor hustle, but neither do they form queues with quite as much enthusiasm as the English. In shops, the assistants are attentive, but not overbearing; they will leave you alone if that is what you want. They are aware of others, but they are often involved with themselves. They rarely shout, but neither do they whisper much. They rarely run, except to catch a train, or to post a letter in the box attached to the backs of trams, though even that stimulus has gone now that these 'moving letter boxes' have been abolished. The old people stroll sedately; the young walk in an upright, but relaxed, way.

In social gatherings, the proprieties are observed. At a reception the sandwiches and the sherry usually appear separately and at a regulated time. You are expected to listen to the speeches and to ask intelligent questions at the appointed time. At formal gatherings in people's homes, the pattern is little different.

Among the upper classes, at least, there is a very English sense of controlled politeness and sometimes the same small cups of tea and thin sandwiches. In most bars and cafés, there is the same sense of controlled restraint. This doesn't mean that you can't have fun and contact in the Netherlands. It is very easy to get into

conversation with Dutch men and women as some 75 per cent of them speak English, many with amazing skill. It is not surprising, perhaps, to find taxi-drivers who speak English, though it is a little more astonishing to find many, as I have done, who can discuss traffic problems, foreign countries, education and other topics with fluency and intelligence. And then there was the tram-driver who told me in very passable English that this was a self-service tram and that I had to stamp my own ticket on the platform at the back. The Dutch dismiss their linguistic abilities with disarming modesty. A young man, training to be a merchant navy officer, who drove a taxi at the week-ends to help out with his budget, told me: 'I suppose it's because I had a very good teacher at school. At one time he had worked in the States as a lawyer. English people tell me that I have a slight American accent.' (He had.) These abilities are so widespread that it's not uncommon to see newspaper advertisements in English and some Dutch people have a habit of ending their telephone conversations with each other in a bewildering mixture of Dutch, English, and even French. They're not showing off; it just comes naturally to them. Most visiting foreigners, and the English in particular, are made to feel welcome in public places. One rainy night in Rotterdam, my wife and I popped into a corner bar for a nightcap before returning to our hotel and emerged an hour or so later having been introduced to almost everyone and having been treated to a Dutch gin. But being invited to a Dutchman's home is more difficult, though not impossible. When you are asked in one night for coffee and cakes you will know that you have arrived.

Even more than in England, the Dutchman's home is his castle.

In 1980, the Dutch spent nearly twice as much on household articles and furnishings as they did on holidays abroad. They spent almost half as much on flowers and plants as they did on buying cars. The windowsills of most Dutch living rooms are so crowded with potted plants and the tables so filled with fragrant displays that foreigners sometimes imagine that they must have entered a florist's shop in error. They also spent much more on books, magazines and newspapers, which are still mainly delivered to the door on a subscription basis, than they did on public entertainment

15

– or tobacco. A recent survey showed that among both men and women, reading was still the favourite spare-time activity at home in 1980, closely followed by watching television, listening to the radio or the hi-fi. But 63 per cent of women and 58 per cent of men also spent some of their leisure time playing cards or other games.

The Dutch are still domestic, home-loving people. The family is the fulcrum of their lives. Letters are quite frequently addressed not to Mr. and Mrs. Jong but to the Jong family. A middle-aged man living abroad will write to his aged mother every week; it is not unusual for a married man to take his father for a week's

Maassluis. 20-3-77

holiday in the summer; mother-in-law is included in the family celebration at a local restaurant.

Family celebrations are the main events in a Dutchman's year. In every house there is a calendar, usually on the back of the kitchen or the lavatory door, with the birthdays not only of the immediate family but also of aunts, uncles, cousins, nephews and nieces carefully noted. The Dutch have two words to describe the family: *gezin,* the closest relatives, and *familie,* the wider circle. Neither of them is neglected in the Netherlands and as many members of the family as possible attend the birthday celebrations. Schoolboys and schoolgirls will invite a few favourite teachers to their birthday parties and in offices, workers subscribe to birthday gifts for their colleagues.

Weddings tend to be more magnificent than in other countries. People who can afford it – and many can – hire a splendid, white carriage and pair to take the bride and bridegroom to the town hall for the civil wedding. Even though the Netherlands is such a religious country, the civil ceremony is the only legal form of marriage; an optional church service may be held afterwards. Before the wedding, there is a stag party for the groom and a 'kitchen shower' for the bride, when her girl friends bring her domestic gifts and have a night's entertainment together. The witnesses of the civil wedding also have the task of organising the 'cabaret' at the reception in the bride's home, which gives a light-hearted view of the couple's lives up to the time of their marriage.

Not so many years ago, receptions were still one- or two-day affairs among the rich. Wedding anniversaries – copper, silver, golden and diamond – are celebrated just as expansively. In one rich family I know they gave each other silver medallions.

Family life is so important to the Dutch that at one time hardly any married women went out to work. As late as 1960, only 3 per cent of all married women, had a full-time job and scarcely any of those had young children. The proportion of married women at work has increased considerably in the last few years. Even so, the proportion of women in the total labour force, just under one-third, is still small compared with other European countries.

The Dutch have always been noted for the cleanliness of their homes and towns: the Dutch word, *schoon,* means both 'clean' and 'beautiful'. Even in the seventeenth century, the wooden bucket and the round-headed mop were always near at hand, as we can see in those delightful Dutch *genre* paintings of that period, such as *A Woman and a Maid in a Courtyard* by Pieter de Hooch. Visitor after visitor, from the seventeenth-century English ambassador, Sir William Temple, onwards commented on 'the great neatness' of their homes, and many foreigners were amazed to find that the Dutch considered it impolite to spit upon the floors as they did at home. Dutch housewives still have a passion for cleaning, dusting, sweeping, scrubbing and mopping, which the furnishing of their homes seems deliberately designed to encourage. There are tile and parquet floors to be cleaned and polished; rugs on tables and sofas to be beaten and banged; potted plants to be tended; and sometimes hundreds of souvenirs and knick-knacks to be dusted. Then there is the washing, most of which is done at home. There are few laundromats in the Netherlands: even in 1964, three-quarters of all homes had washing machines. And there is also the shopping, the cooking, the sewing . . . The housewife does most of her work unaided. There are few domestic servants, and husbands, particularly in the older-age groups, are not expected to help with domestic tasks, though attitudes are different among the younger generation. But in some homes, the housewife still cleans the family's shoes.

Family life, however, is not so backward and old-fashioned as it may seem. The Dutch have adapted to the modern pattern of family life just as easily and as successfully as people in other industrialised countries. But the Dutch have been determined to retain the cosy, comfortable elements of domestic life which they have always loved: they have their own word, *gezellig,* to describe this quality, which is virtually untranslatable, and certainly unpronounceable by most foreigners!

The Dutch have been more successful than many other nations in maintaining close links with the extended family of aunts, uncles and in-laws. (That is one of the reasons for the popularity of telephones in the Netherlands, which are now installed in nine out of ten homes, one of the higher ratios in the world.) Financially, too, the husband and the wife are more of a partnership than in some other industrialised countries. By law, neither of them may sell or let part of their house, make excessive gifts to other people,

Amsterdam

J. DALENOORD

or sign hire-purchase agreements without the other's consent. The Dutch live the way they do because they like it and not because they know no other way. They are true conservationists and conservatives (in the non-political sense), retaining all that is worth-while and appealing from the past.

So much has altered, yet so much is still unchanged. That, for

me at least, is one of the major delights of the country. Little of any real value is lost. Going back to the Netherlands is always like re-entering some warm, cosy room. In the streets, there are still the same bicycles – eleven million in all, plus another million mopeds – which are fit for a queen and therefore for everyone. There are still those ornately-decorated barrel organs – six in Amsterdam alone – and those same stalls selling raw or salted herring which, Dutch gourmets say, should be swallowed, like oysters, not chewed. There are still the same cosy brown bars and cafés, with their dark panelled walls, their shaded lights and their tables covered with heavy rugs, just as tables have always been covered from the seventeenth century when Dutch merchants brought rugs back from the Middle East. In the last two or three years, many Englishmen have felt even more at home in Dutch bars, since many of them have installed a darts board, a game which the Dutch have taken up with great enthusiasm. These small, warm, intimate cafés do not supplant the home but duplicate it, just as the merchants' houses by the canals reflect the same image in the water as they did in those seventeenth-century *genre* paintings.

What gives the country its atmosphere and its aesthetic appeal is the concentration of fine detail. Space has always been a precious commodity here. If the Dutch had not dammed the rivers, diked the sea and drained the land about half of the country would still lie under water. The saving of space, the arranging of objects in symmetrical harmony is one of the country's major characteristics. Look at any street! One in the old, semi-circular heart of Amsterdam, ringed by its concentric canals, will do. At first sight it looks uniformly elegant with its rows of tall merchants' houses facing the canals. All the houses are built of small bricks and are only faced with stone, which has always been scarce in the Netherlands

20

and has, therefore, to be imported. None of the houses is dominant; but a closer inspection reveals the mass of fine, individual detail. Each house has a beautiful gable, but every one is individual. Some of the gables are geometrically stepped; others are shaped like a bell, a bottle or a triangle. The gables were not mere decoration. Each has a hoist, which was used to haul goods up to the upper storeys, which were sometimes used by the merchants as their warehouse. If you look closely, you will see that some of the houses lean forward slightly, appearing to bow to the houses across the canals. No! The wooden piles on which they were built are not faltering! The houses were built in that way so that the

bulky bundles would not damage the brickwork as they were hauled aloft.

Steep flights of stone steps lead up to the front door. There is an iron handrail supported on slender balustrades, which matches the railings along the side of the canal and the more sturdy iron bollard for tying up the merchant's barges. The pavement slopes a little irregularly, giving each cobblestone its individual slant. The road humps over the canal. No surface is unbroken, no space is wasted here: from the walls of the canals hang wooden boxes containing flowers. The attention to detail is continued and repeated inside the houses. On the window sill, there is a row of potted plants interspersed with knick-knacks – strangely-shaped shells, paperweights, a piece of coral, miniature vases – small, but to the Dutch, strangely significant things.

The Dutch have always loved small objects. In the Rijksmuseum in Amsterdam and in other museums elsewhere, many examples can be seen of these exquisite early seventeenth-century Dutch cabinets on stands. Some are covered with tortoiseshell over red foil; others have painted panels with biblical or rural scenes commissioned by the purchaser. In the small drawers of the cabinet, the owner kept his hoard of personally precious things – lenses, stones, exotic shells – many of which had been brought back by sailors from the newly-explored Orient. The same passion is revealed in the Dutch still-life paintings of the seventeenth century with their arrangements of common, everyday objects – a comb, a newspaper, a knife, a key, a watch, a piece of sealing wax. It is displayed too in the Dutch interiors of the same period, in the paintings of Jan Steen, of Johannes Vermeer, of Pieter de Hooch and many others. The objects are diverse, but commonplace, whether it is a painting of a merchant's house or of a peasant's home. Scattered on the floor there is a seemingly haphazard collection of everyday objects – a bowl, a shoe, an apple, a mallet. The family's pet dog is also often included, as the Dutch loved animals then as they do to this day, when they provide roadside 'comfort stations' for dogs and, in one place at least, a traffic sign warning motorists to beware of ducks crossing the road from a nearby pond! The floor is often the focal point of the painting. No less than the familiar objects themselves it represents some security.

The Dutch have always had an interest in small detail, in substance rather than show. Although there are still, and always have been, visionaries among the Dutch, this passion for detail has persisted to the present day. It is firmly embedded in the Dutch character. They like things to be well ordered and well arranged, to have everything – and everyone – in its proper place. This necessity has been forced on them by their history. The hostile physical environment and early development of overcrowded towns forced them to become planners many centuries ago. Even in the seventeenth century an estimated 50 per cent of the population of the province of Holland lived in towns, a proportion which was not reached in England until the nineteenth century and in France until the late 1920s.

For the Dutchman, no stone must ever be left unturned. That is why the Dutch can seem to be such hard bargainers: no detail is too small to remain unexamined; no small defect must be left unexposed. 'It's not really surprising that we should be this way,' an Amsterdam insurance broker told me. 'We've been wheeling and dealing all over the world for many centuries. It's habit you find hard to give up – like smoking.' The Dutch have never been able to afford to make mistakes, but they are honest and fair in their dealings with others. Their ears are usually open to further discussions.

The same concentration on detail can sometimes lead to hairsplitting arguments and discussions: whether one car should be taken or two, whether a tunnel or a bridge should be built. It is in such areas that the Dutch like to dwell. This trait encourages them to form breakaway political parties, religious sects and rival groupings. The significance of detail also helps to create their sense of earnestness: there are many problems all of equal weight on their mind. But how can this be reconciled with their barely-concealed sense of humour and the pervasive feeling of warm humanity?

It is dangerous to generalise about any nation, but there does seem to be an essential duality in the Dutch. They appear to be earnest, conformist, a little rigid and sometimes even disputatious, which some foreigners often mistakenly believe is their whole character. Inside, however, there is always a warm, expansive individual waiting to burst out.

23

Nowhere is this duality better illustrated than in the Amstelkring Museum of Our Lord in the Attic in Amsterdam. From the outside, this museum looks little different from the neighbouring seventeenth-century merchants' houses. Indeed, that is what it once was – three houses built by a hosier, Jan Hartman, in 1661. The living room has a plain classical simplicity and symmetry, with its tall, well-proportioned windows, its panelled ceiling, its heavy furniture, its walnut cupboard-bed and its religious paintings and its portraits. Only the ornately-twisted marble columns of the solid, monumental mantelpiece give any clue to what will be found upstairs.

Climbing up the narrow stairs to the attic, which extends the whole length and breadth of the three adjoining houses, you find a concealed chapel, breathtaking in its unexpected baroque beauty of blue and gold, with adoring angels and sanctuary lamp cast in solid silver. The chapel was built after the war of independence against Spain in the early 17th century, when Catholicism was still officially proscribed in the Netherlands, though the city fathers of Amsterdam, with a traditional tolerance, turned a blind eye to such chapels of which there were once twenty-six in the capital alone.

For me, this place has come to symbolise the country in a number of different ways. There is first of all the tolerance and the sense of religion. There is the austere, rather cold, beauty of the living room contrasted with the concealed warm splendour of the chapel. And there is the Dutchman living with his feet firmly planted on the ground, but with his head in the clouds: the pragmatic man and the visionary combined.

With the great importance of family life, it is not surprising that

housing should have been one of the main matters of concern in the post-war years. Since the last war about three million homes have been built, but as in most industrialised countries there are still not enough houses of the right kind, in the right place and at the right price. Most large cities have long waiting lists for council flats and houses. Students, young couples, and some immigrants find it particularly difficult to obtain suitable accommodation at a price they can afford. Rents of unfurnished accommodation are controlled, though they have been rising rather steeply in the last few years while property speculation in the 1970s (some of it by British companies) has sent house prices soaring. Many Dutch people are painfully aware of the defects of their post-war apartments, though a recent survey has shown that they were more content with their houses in 1980 than they were six years before. Almost everyone has his own favourite tale of the intolerable trials of life in a new apartment block: the thin walls through which every whisper can be heard; the noise of young children playing in the flat above and of the teenager with his transistor in

J. DALENOORD

the flat below; of doors that do not shut firmly; of cupboards which are too small; of enforced encounters with other people on the common balcony. In most big cities there are lines of houseboats moored on the canals and areas of sub-standard housing such as those old houses with small backyards and tin or plastic baths hanging on the outside walls, which is what the traveller by train sees first as he approaches Rotterdam from the south, though these were being demolished in the summer of 1982.

The Dutch, however, are more self-critical about their housing than they need be. A house or a flat in Amsterdam or The Hague, which the Dutch find scandalously expensive, would cost more to rent or to buy in London. Neighbour noise is now an international problem which afflicts most city dwellers. Although some of the houseboats are rather decrepit old barges which have been converted into homes because no other accommodation is available, many more are comfortable, well-furnished dwellings with permanent supplies of electricity and running water. With typical Dutch inventiveness, many occupants have converted their decks into roof gardens with strategically-scattered tubs of plants and flowers. Other houseboats are occupied by Dutch students or 'drop-outs' from other countries, who have bought an old, cheap barge and converted it into a psychedelic 'paradise'. None of them is any worse than the colonies of caravan homes, or what are euphemistically called mobile homes, to be found on the outskirts of cities in Britain and the United States. The Netherlands is not the only country to have sub-standard houses; they are to be found in their thousands in many British and American cities. What the Dutchman calls a 'slum', the English or American visitor would describe as a few streets, or blocks, of rather bleak and cheerless homes. The unique structure of the *Randstad,* a massive, post-war reconstruction programme, and the restoration and conservation of old houses and of whole urban areas, such as the Jordaan in Amsterdam, has restricted inner city blight and decay. The Dutch have done more than many other nations in western Europe to preserve their architectural heritage and many of their old, seventeenth-century houses have been beautifully restored to their original state. Since 1961 the government has actively encouraged and financially supported people in this task. Owners can obtain grants of up to 70 per cent from the public purse to help meet the costs of restoring houses, churches, windmills and other buildings. Buildings which have been put on the protected list of the Ministry of Culture, Recreation and Social Welfare cannot be pulled down or altered in any way, without permission. Avenues of trees, favourite views in towns and in the countryside can be preserved in the same way. No less than forty thousand buildings are on the Ministry's list, about one in two hundred of all buildings in the country. As any tourist would expect, seven thousand of these buildings are in Amsterdam, but many other cities and towns have their share. For example, the little coastal town of Harlingen in Friesland has no less than five hundred. Restoration costs can be enormous. One old house that I visited in Haarlem had cost nearly £ 750,000 (1,275,000 dollars) to restore. In 1980, the Ministry of Culture alone gave grants totalling £ 30 million (54 million dollars) for restoration work. The Dutch think it is money well spent.

Orvelte, Drente

It means that the historic heart of their cities will be preserved for all time, not as a dead museum, but as a living, and lived-in, example of the past. The Ministry encourages ordinary people to report any threat to buildings over fifty years old which might be worth preserving.

I was discussing this very point with an official of the Department for the Preservation of Monuments and Historic Buildings in Zeist, in a building which in itself is a supreme example of the restorer's and conservationist's art, when her telephone rang.

'That was a man from Groningen,' she told me when she returned. 'He's worried that a row of eight old houses will be pulled down if a new municipal plan is passed, and wanted to know what he could do about it.'

'Do you get many calls like that?' I asked.

'Oh, yes, the phone's ringing all day long. We could do much more to help if we only had more money. But in this case, that wasn't the problem. They can pay for it themselves.'

Although many of the old houses have been converted into offices, some are still occupied by families. They make delightful homes with their tall, well-proportioned rooms, large windows, and enclosed gardens or courtyards. One house that I visited in Amsterdam had been renovated and restored by a senior civil servant. The drawing room was furnished with splendid antique chests and cupboards, chairs and tables – heirlooms of the family. On a mezzanine floor there was a small private courtyard filled with flowers and plants. The bathroom was modern, a striking contrast of black and white. And at tree-top level there was a studio, stretching the whole length of the house, with a glass-shelved structure at one end to contain those small objects – shells, vases, stones – so greatly loved by the Dutch. It was a really delightful home.

Only a handful of people, unfortunately, can live in these beautiful

homes. Space was a precious commodity, even in the seventeenth century when these houses were built, so that the merchants' houses along the Herengracht, the Keizersgracht and the Prinsengracht in Amsterdam were not allowed to have a frontage more than three windows wide. Space is still scarce to this day, so that allotments are squeezed in beside the embankments of railways and sheep graze on the banks of suburban canals. Escalators in modern stores and staircases in private homes tend to rise more steeply and to be less wide than elsewhere. The Dutch have become used to it as any visitor will realize when he sees a Dutchman scale a flight of almost perpendicular stairs, with two heavy suitcases in his hands, as easily and as effortlessly as you or I walk across a room. Most Dutch people have a yearning for wide open spaces. They would prefer to have a house of their own with a garden and a sandpit for their children, but it is not so easy to find except in remote country districts. There are, however, many lucky people even in the crowded *Randstad,* who have a chance to get away whenever they like by walking down to the bottom of their garden, where their dinghy or small cabin cruiser is moored by the bank of a canal. But the majority of people have

Zoetermeer

to live in modern terraced houses or apartment blocks. After the war, the Dutch built many small, pleasant blocks of flats of only four or five storeys, with traditional large picture windows looking out on to communal gardens and play areas. They also experimented with more unconventional designs which have been encouraged since 1968 by special government subsidies. Dr. Fieldeldij Dop, one of the country's best-known child psychologists, helped to found an organisation – New Living Forms – with architects, builders, social workers and others to build houses fit for people, instead of houses in which people can fit. It has already built some houses at Eindhoven, with open spaces outside the homes instead of gardens, and open spaces inside with many large nooks instead of dividing walls.

The demand for housing, however, was so great that the Dutch were forced, a little reluctantly perhaps, to adopt the international, post-war pattern of the highrise. By 1968 almost half of the apartment blocks being built had nine storeys or more. As a result, the big cities, like those in other European countries, were encircled by huge concrete suburbs, or satellite towns. The latest one at Amsterdam is being built at Bijlmermeer, connected with the city centre by a new underground railway. Eventually, it will house a hundred thousand people, mainly in eleven-storey-high blocks.

At first sight, it has the same chilling appearance as other new towns, but the planners have made a real attempt to create reasonable living patterns for the mass-consumption age. From the air the huge concrete blocks form themselves into the shape of a honeycomb, with their open ends enclosing vast cells of rolling parkland, trees and lakes. The buildings are three hundred and sixty feet apart, or more, to reduce neighbour noise and to ensure that the occupants can look out from their picture windows on to a green foreground of trees and flowering shrubs instead of concrete slabs and paths. There will be a central park of about 125 acres, bigger than Vondel park in the heart of Amsterdam. To preserve the peace, all motor traffic (apart from ambulances, police cars and fire engines) is banned from the whole area. Bijlmermeer can be reached by motorways, which are raised ten feet above the ground, but all cars have to be left in the communal car parks, which are connected to the blocks of flats by enclosed walkways. Similar causeways, at first floor level, connect each block to other buildings in the development; the ground floors are used for storage, and cycle and pedestrian paths. The majority of the flats have four rooms, plus a kitchen and a bathroom, though there are some smaller flats, and a few with five or six rooms. All the flats are centrally heated. This is certainly a bold and imaginative scheme, though it is too early to say whether it will provide what people really want. With the great increase in the population of the Netherlands in the post-war years, developments of this kind were almost inevitable. For many years the country has had one of the lowest death rates in the world, only 8.0 per thousand in 1981. Until recently, the birthrate was one of the highest in western Europe. As a result mainly of these demographic factors, the population increased steadily from just over 10 million in 1950, to nearly 11½ million in 1960 to just under 13 million in 1970. If things had gone on in that way, there would have been nearly 20 million Dutch people by the year 2000, so that the fall in the birthrate from 17.2 per thousand in 1971 to 12.6 per thousand ten years later has caused the authorities to heave a sigh of relief. The population on December 31, 1981, was 14,340,000. By the year 2000 it is now expected to be only 15,400,000. Nevertheless, there will still be a shortage of land for all the nation's needs building houses, making parks, growing crops so that the Dutch are still creating more land for themselves.

Sooner or later, when writing about the Netherlands, one always

has to come back to the subject of land reclamation. The cities in the *Randstad* are literally built on sand, as you can see if you look under any dislodged paving stone or peer into any excavation for a new building. So much has been said, and written, about the subject, that the story has lost much of its impact. But the centuries-long struggle of the Dutch to master the sea is really a most remarkable achievement, a continuing saga. The more so, because this peaceful conquest of land takes place without ever becoming an infringement of any other state's sovereign rights! Today the Netherlands is renowned for the neat geometrical appearance of its landscape; but two thousand years ago much of it was a wild, untamed, desolate region which terrified even the invading Romans. Their ships were often struck at night by huge floating trees uprooted from the banks of lakes and rivers; the masts became entangled in the branches. In the south-west, the great European rivers of the Rhine and the Maas (the Meuse) created a huge swampy delta, a region of large and small islands, lakes and shifting dunes of sand shaken ceaselessly, like some giant kaleidoscope, into new patterns by the waves and winds of the North Sea. In the north the sand dunes were frequently breached and broken by the incursions of the sea, creating the chain of small isolated Frisian islands, separated from the mainland by the shallow Wadden Sea. On the mainland there was a low-lying peaty swamp, with hundreds of small lakes, some of them created by peasants who dug up the peat for fuel and used the salty ashes for preserving fish and meat.

For many centuries the Dutch have struggled to create a new land out of the sea, at first, in northern Friesland, with their bare hands, wicker baskets and primitive sledges. Over the course of many years, the Frisians built huge mounds of earth, called terpen, some of which were 40 acres in extent. Pliny, the Roman historian, who visited the region in A.D. 47, described how the inhabitants resembled 'sailors in ships when the water covers the surrounding land, but shipwrecked people when the tide was retired.' Later, dikes, or sea walls, were built to protect the land from flooding. They had a flap gate which let water flow out into the sea at low tide and stopped it coming in at high tide. (The story of the boy with his finger in the dike is a colourful invention of the nineteenth-century American writer, Mary Mapes Dodge, though in the 1953 floods some brave villagers of Colijnsplaat, on North Beveland, did put their shoulders to a wall of sandbags in a dike to prevent the water from pushing the bags away.)

At the beginning of the fifteenth century windmills started to come into use. The sails of the mills transferred their rotation force, obtained from the wind, to scoop wheels with buckets attached which carried the excess water away from the drainage ditches and discharged it into a ring-canal around the reclaimed land, so that it could be discharged into the sea. The early windmills could raise water only five feet, so three windmills were sometimes built together, as you can still see in places, to raise water to a higher level of approximately fifteen feet. There were

also industrial windmills which were used for many different purposes including grinding wheat, sawing wood, turning rags into paper and grinding snuff and spices. The windmills were also used as primitive semaphore stations. Messages could be sent for miles across the flat, open countryside by altering the position of the wings or sails. When one pair of sails were exactly vertical and the other pair were horizontal, it indicated that the mill was ready to start work. A slight turn of the sails backwards indicated a birth; a slight turn onwards, a death. For marriages or other celebrations, the sails were gaily decorated with flags, rosettes, hearts made of tin plate and angels blowing trumpets.
In the nineteenth century the windmills were gradually replaced

dike-farmhouse, river Lek

by steampumps and there are now modern diesel or electric pumping stations which each can pump over 3 million litres of water a minute.

There are still about a thousand windmills in the country, of which three hundred or so are used for pumping water or making flour though the Dutch no longer need to use them for either purpose. But the Dutch have a great affection for their windmills, which has been strengthened by the recent campaign to preserve their unique architectural inheritance. A year or so ago the inhabitants of the little town of Nijeveen in Drenthe realised that they had a great problem. They had a *Molenstraat* (Mill street) in their town but no windmill. They knew that no other town or village in the Netherlands would be willing to give them one, so they had the bright idea of getting one from Germany. They brought it back and rebuilt it piece by piece. And now they're all delighted to have a windmill in their *Molenstraat* again, even though it is only German and not Dutch!

The Dutch people have an equal affection, though some of them won't admit it, for those famous fields of tulips around Haarlem and Leiden which cover the earth with a patchwork quilt of colour in the spring. And even wooden shoes strike some chord of history in the Dutch, though you will not see many clogs outside the souvenir shops except on some farms and in some gardens in the north. (I did once see a road workman wearing a pair in Leeuwarden, the capital of Friesland.) Clogs, tulips and windmills have become a stock image of the Netherlands for many foreigners, and though the Dutch don't mind that too much, accepting it with a good-humoured tolerance, what they really do resent, and quite rightly too, is the lingering idea that there is nothing else. Even their spectacular technical success in reclaiming land should have been sufficient in itself to destroy any remnant of the old-fashioned image of the country.

The Dutch have been reclaiming land from the sea for hundreds

of years, but it is only in this century that modern technology has enabled them almost to manipulate the sea at will. (They know far too much about the sea, however, to treat it lightly.) The first major project was the draining of the former Zuyder Zee, which

involved the construction of a nineteen-mile-long barrier dam
connecting the provinces of North Holland and Friesland. Since
1932 you have been able to drive by car along the road on the top
of the dam, which is one of the most unusual in Europe, with sea
on one side and a freshwater lake – IJsselmeer – on the other.
Most of the remainder of the seabed, some half-a-million acres in
all, has been pumped dry to create four enormous polders of
reclaimed land.

For those people who live nearby, and Amsterdam is right on the
doorstep, it has been like watching the creation of part of the
world in less than a lifetime. When a polder first starts to emerge
from the water it is a bleak and depressing sight. I shall never
forget the first time I saw the polder of South Flevoland. It was

Hoge Beintum, Friesland

winter and the snow still lay lightly on the bleak wastes of sludge and mud, interspersed with pools of water, which stretched as far as the wreaths of swirling mist would allow the eye to see. If I ignored the car in which my friend had brought me, and the occasional sound of a passing lorry or car, it was just as it must have been in the beginning when the land rose from the sea. There were no animals, no birds, not even any insects. Only the relics of vanished civilisations, lying somewhere in that vast expanse of mud, would have shown that people had lived there centuries

Zuid- Holland Stompwijk

before: the wooden beams and broken spires of churches which had disappeared below the sea, the shipwrecked boats and, at a deeper level, the bones of prehistoric animals and the remains of human skeletons, some of them dating from 2500 B.C. But the former sea bed was still too wet and treacherous for me to walk on it.

The first stage in transforming this barren muddy waste into land fit for crops and people is to sow it with reed seeds from planes and helicopters. The reeds suck up the moisture, while the sun and air help to dry out the soil. These activities attract other forms of life. As the land is being drained, gulls fly in from the coast to investigate; the swampy reeds become a breeding ground for midges, flies and bees. After a year the reeds are cut down and burnt. The land is ploughed and sown with rape seed, whose oil can be used for making margarine. This is followed by cereal crops. As the land is cultivated, animals move in. Mice and voles arrive and attract their natural enemy, the kestrel. Larger animals, rabbits and deer, cross the frozen waters of the lakes in winter to stake out their claims in the new land. Grass and fast-growing trees, such as willows and poplars, are planted; roads are built; fields are formed; farmers' houses are constructed.

Soon there is very little to indicate that all of this is not as nature intended apart from the straightness of the roads and the regularity of the fields. From the air the polders look like an exercise in geometry, or an abstract painting with a yellow background, split up into squares and rectangles by straight strokes of green, on which blobs of blue have been superimposed.

Originally, the main purpose of the Zuyder Zee works, apart

from flood prevention, was to provide more agricultural land and to create a fresh water lake. After the Second World War, with the growth of population and changes in the economy, it was decided to make more use of the new land for recreation and housing. Trees were planted to provide wooded areas with picnic sites; the shores of lakes were kinked to give them a more natural appearance. A new town, called Lelystad after Cornelius Lely who thought up the scheme, has been built in the East Flevoland polder. In 1977 work had already started on another overspill town, Almere, which is being built on the adjoining polder of South Flevoland. The final polder, Markerwaard, was originally due to be finished by 1980, but at the time of writing it is still a vast sheet of water. The Dutch haven't quite made up their minds what they want to do with Markerwaard so they've paused for thought and discussion. A few people wanted it to be used for farming; others believed it should be used for housing; while still more thought it should be used for recreation or partly for the construction of a second, national airport. There was no real consensus. The latest idea is that about a third of it could be made into a 50,000-acre lake and the other 100,000 acres could be reclaimed for agricultural use and possibly for housing. But it would be an expensive project. The basic cost of reclaiming the land would be nearly £300 million (540 million dollars) at 1980 prices – and many conservationists still remain opposed to the project. Environmental pressure groups are extremely powerful in the Netherlands. In the south-west of the country an equally ambitious scheme – the Delta project – was started after the disastrous floods of February 1953. It has involved damming several estuaries in the Zeeland and South Holland islands and erecting a storm-tide barrier in the Hollandse IJssel near Rotterdam. The barrier has a massive steel gate, weighing 635 tons, which is suspended between two tall towers and which can be lowered if

Delta works

there is any danger of a flood tide coming upstream from the North Sea. New techniques have been used for building the dams. Hundreds of tons of imported stone or home-made concrete blocks have been dropped from overhead cableways on to the river bed, and huge concrete caissons have been towed into position by tugs and then flooded so that they sink to form a dam. Work had already started on the last and biggest dam across the five-mile-wide Eastern Scheldt, when the environmentalists raised their voices in protest again. They said that if the work went ahead, the unique flora and fauna and wildlife of the tidal reaches, and the remaining oyster and mussel beds, would be lost for ever. Their campaign to save the Eastern Scheldt had a great impact not only in Zeeland itself but also in other parts of the country.

'One of the big advantages of living in a small country,' a journalist told me, 'is that ideas can spread like crazy. If you live in The Hague and have some idea that you want other people to support, you can be in the far north explaining it to the people of Groningen within a couple of hours.' The government, which is always ready to listen to new ideas, too, took the objections seriously. It asked its officials and technical staff how the Eastern Scheldt could be kept open so that the natural environment would be preserved and yet be closed in times of danger to give perfect safety.

That was some problem, as it had never been tackled anywhere in the world before. But the Dutch have come up with a solution. A sluice dam is being built, with eighty separate openings about 130 feet wide, which will let most of the tidal waters through in normal times but which can be closed with heavy steel gates whenever a severe storm threatens. It will cost an extra £ 800 million (1,440 million dollars) in addition to the costs of maintenance and the whole project will not be completed until 1985. The Dutch are prepared to wait, and to pay, if they can preserve what nature has provided over the course of many centuries and, thereby, improve the quality of life. They are all conservationists now. That is why it is almost certain that they will never go ahead with an earlier plan to reclaim the Wadden Sea, which separates the Frisian islands from the mainland. (You can walk across at low tide, but if you try it, please take a Frisian as a guide. It is still a rather risky experiment!)

The Wadden Sea area is renowned as one of the most important bird sanctuaries in western Europe. It is one of the major stop-over points on the migratory route from the Arctic circle to southern Europe, Africa and the Antarctic. Hundreds of different species of birds can be seen there including the Barnacle Goose, the eider, the avocet, the oystercatcher, the sandwich tern, the golden plover and the snow bunting. The environmentalists believe it is important to preserve this bird sanctuary, with its additional opportunities for sailing and fishing, and the unique quality of its island life. Although the Dutch now have the technical skill to alter the balance of land and water in this confident way, the main task remains, as it always has been, to protect the country from the sea. Without the dikes, the dunes, and the pumping stations, about half the country would be flooded twice a day. The coastline would stretch from Groningen in the north, through Zwolle, Utrecht, Arnhem and Den Bosch to Breda in the south, and many of the major cities in the *Randstad* would be under water.

Kagerplas

Town-life is associated inevitably with the Netherlands,

as the Dutch were among the first people in northern Europe to develop well-run, civilised cities for the people. Amsterdam was the final example of that long medieval line of city-states stretching back to Venice and Florence. Most of the best architecture is to be found in the cities: the merchants' houses, the churches as big as cathedrals, and the town halls. There are also some fine castles on the eastern border, in the centre around Utrecht, and in the southern province of Limburg which has no less than a hundred. There is also variety and a beauty of its own kind in the countryside. The western and northern parts are flat. The only thing the Dutch rarely provide in their land reclamation schemes is hills, though there is one in the man-made woods of Amsterdamse Bos in the capital. The flat landscape – a Dutch word, *landschap,* in origin – has an immensity and power of its own. It conceals nothing. On clear days you can see for miles.

Every detail is distinct. In contrast to the crowded cities, there is a great sense of solitude and silence. There is something very fundamental about the landscape, a feeling of being close to the origins of nature, with the sense that the earth is only a fragile covering of the waters of the sea and that the over-arching sky, flecked with clouds, is very close. The Dutch are affected just as powerfully as foreigners by this unique countryside. Either they love its powerful isolation or they find it somewhat bare and monotonous.

The Netherlands is not all flat and man-made. In the north-east there is the quiet province of Drenthe with its small towns and heather-covered moors where sheep may safely graze. Nearer the centre, there is the province of Gelderland where the roads rise up towards the wooded heights of the National Park of Hooge Veluwe, with its red deer, wild boar, and the Kröller-Müller museum containing sculptures and van Goghs. Further south there are the provinces of North Brabant and Limburg, where the countryside is softer and takes on a more natural shape than in the west. As you drive south, you will notice that the pastures become rougher, rising into little hillocks and falling into what were once small pools; the streams and rivers wind, choosing a course they have evolved through the centuries. The trees grow naturally and in haphazard clumps and not only in planned places. The vision is held and contained by a line of low wooded hills on the horizon.

Considering that it takes less than four hours to travel by train from the north of the country to the south, there is a remarkable variety of scenery and regional differences. Friesland in the north has its own very distinctive character. The Frisians have their own language, which is now taught in all schools; their own flag; and even their own anthem, the *Frysk Folksliet*. But there is no political movement for separation from the rest of the Netherlands, but only for greater cultural autonomy. They have their own special drinks, and their own sports: pole-vaulting over canals; *kaatsen*, a game played by three-man teams; and the gruelling 125-mile skating race across the frozen canals and lakes which join the eleven towns of the province.

Friesland is very different from the southernmost province of Limburg, which juts down between Germany and the French-speaking part of Belgium. Foreign influences flow across the frontiers. French words appear above the shops; more wine is drunk; and even the meat in butcher's shops is cut differently. Around Sittard, the spacious Dutch windows start to shrink into a smaller size and some of the houses have steep, Germanic roofs with red rounded tiles and roof ridges running parallel to the street, instead of at right angles as in most other Dutch towns. In spite of these differences, there is a distinctive feeling of Dutchness in all the provinces. Unlike many other European countries, there are no great separatist movements in the Netherlands. What holds these diverse people together? Throughout the centuries the Dutch have learnt to live with each other and with their differences. 'So long as other people don't bother us,' a lecturer in history explained to me, 'we don't want to bother others. We've always had enough problems of our own, like keeping back the sea and making a living. They're quite enough!'

The Dutch became a nation long before they set up a unified state at the beginning of the nineteenth century. During the Dutch republic, which lasted from the seventeenth century to the end of the eighteenth century, each city, each province guarded its own autonomy jealously. The Dutch people still remain attached to their provinces in sentiment, speech and attitudes, but they are also patriotic, rather than nationalistic, relating to the whole country through the symbols of national unity of which they are so proud: the Royal family; the Dutch airline KLM, the oldest airline in the world operating under its original name; and the flood prevention schemes and the welfare state, to which they all contribute through their taxes.

As in other industrial countries, there are now increasing similarities between the regions. The motor-car and the television set are enemies of provincialism. The road across the enclosing dam in the north has helped to bring Friesland and Groningen into more

Thorn

immediate contact with the *Randstad,* just as the new roads across the dams in the south-west delta are helping to force some of the islands of Zeeland and South Holland out of their former isolation. Industry has spread to many towns and cities outside the *Randstad.* In the south there is the city of Eindhoven, which was only a small village when the Philips brothers started to make electric light bulbs there at the end of the nineteenth century. Since then, other industries have moved in, including Daf truck manufacturers, which has recently increased its share in a diminishing world market and scored a special success in the Middle East with its new range of hot-weather lorries. Daf car manufacturers, a separate organisation, which is now part of the Swedish Volvo group, has its headquarters at Helmond, a few miles east of Eindhoven. In spite of the recession, it also succeeded in increasing its sales by ten per cent in 1981. A more recent Dutch arrival in the area is Holecsol Systems, which specialises in solar panels, cells and pumps. Some foreign firms have also opened factories recently in Eindhoven, including the American Spectra Physics, which makes industrial and scientific lasers. But the marks of the founders are still very evident in the town. The electronic train indicators on the railway platforms are made by Philips. The enormous figure of Jesus rising up above the spire of the main church is illuminated at night by Philips lamps. In the modern hotels, some of which are owned by Philips, there is always much talk of sales figures and lengthy anecdotes about computers and company personnel. This huge multinational company, with 370,000 employees world wide, has given Eindhoven such a great international reputation, that the town has recently been nominated World Trade Centre Electronics. A headquarters is being built, which will house permanent exhibitions and data banks to provide the latest information on all aspects of the new technology. Tourists from many parts of the world are also attracted there by the company's *Evoluon,* a spectacular flying-saucer-shaped exhibition hall held aloft by slender concrete pillars, with graphic displays inside showing the impact of electronics on modern life and man.

There are other industrial towns, too – Arnhem, Breda, Tilburg, for example – but in spite of this dispersal, there are still not enough industries outside the *Randstad.*

For many centuries the Dutch have been among the most efficient

farmers in the world. During the seventeenth century Royalist farmers fled from England to the Netherlands and to Flanders which is now in the northern, Dutch-speaking part of Belgium. Farmers there on the 'barrenest, Heathie and Sandie lands' were already growing magnificent crops of oats and providing winter feed and lush pastures for their cattle by sowing turnips and clover. When the exiles returned to England after the Restoration they, too, started growing clover and planting turnips on light soils, ushering in the English agricultural revolution long before the famous, but now discredited, 'Turnip' Townshend was even born. In the same century Dutch engineers, such as Cornelius Vermuyden, were being employed to drain the Fens around Cambridge in England to create more farming land.

The Dutch have long been agricultural innovators. The modern steel and galvanised-iron Dutch barn can be seen in many different parts of the world. On some farms in the Netherlands you can see the modern version and the original model side by side. It has a thatched roof, supported by four stout poles at each corner, which can be raised or lowered to protect the hay beneath.

The Dutch have a long tradition in food processing extending from salted herring, once a staple food in Europe, which was introduced by Willem Beukels of Zeeland in the fourteenth century, to margarine which was first extensively produced in the Netherlands in the nineteenth century.

These traditions continue to this day. The black and white Frisian cow, which gives the highest milk yield in the world, has been exported to many different countries. Much Dutch milk is exported in a processed form as butter, cheese, condensed and powdered milk. Gouda and Edam cheeses are eaten in many foreign countries and just recently, some of the Dutch speciality cheeses, such as Leidsekaas, containing caraway seeds, have also become available in foreign shops. (Unfortunately, you will rarely find cheese on the dinner menu in Dutch restaurants, as it is eaten in the Netherlands only at breakfast and lunch time or as a snack with drinks, when it is cut up into little cubes which some Dutchmen like to dip in mustard.)

Dutch skills in growing flowers and bulbs extend back over many centuries. Their passions for tulips and the profits that could be made from rare varieties led to a financial speculation in the 1630s – tulipomania – which bankrupted many dealers when the bubble burst.

The Dutch have made up for it since. In 1980 the turnover of the cut flower industry was about £ 250 million (450 million dollars) and the bulb industry was worth another £ 70 million (126 million dollars). The Dutch like to make sure that their flowers are as fresh as possible. The wrapping paper is often stamped with the date when they were picked. Although the Dutch are sometimes accused by foreigners of being mean, their magnificent bunches of flowers are more than generous in size and quantity of unopened blooms and extremely cheap by international standards. They make the perfect gift for your hostess when you are invited into a

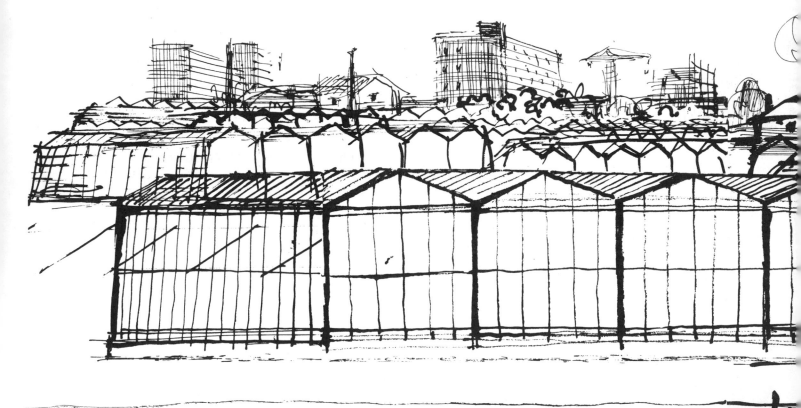

Westland

Dutch home. Flowers for export are picked in the evening;
auctioned the following morning; and flown out of Schiphol
airport by KLM so that they can be sold in New York and other
big cities in the world on the same day. The unique Dutch
auction, which is much quicker than traditional methods, helps to
speed up the process. Bidding prices, which are shown on a large
clock, start at a high level and rapidly descend. The first dealer to
press his button becomes the buyer. This system is also used at the
other hundred and twenty auctions where tomatoes, cucumbers,
lettuce and other vegetables are sold, mainly for export.
Horticulture plays a significant part in the Dutch economy.
Nearly twenty per cent of agricultural land is given over to
horticulture, of which nearly half is under glass. Dutch skills were

J. DALENOORD

vividly illustrated at the Floriade exhibition which was held on the outskirts of Amsterdam for 186 days in 1982. This spectacular show was a riot of colour from the opening displays of tulips and other bulbs in April, through displays of orchids, roses, lilies, gladioli and dahlias to the final flurry of autumn flowers, vegetables and fruit in October. Every aspect of horticulture, including bee-keeping, allotments, herbs, energy-saving and much more, was covered on the 138-acre site, which could be seen on foot by the industrious or from a little electric train for those who wanted an easy ride. This biggest exhibition of its kind takes so long to prepare and to plant out, that there will be no chance to see the next one until 1992.

Statistics and impressions, however, can be misleading. Many small farms have been unable to survive within the framework of the European Economic Community. Some fruit farmers have been unable to compete with the more favourably situated Italian and French farmers. Farms have been engrossed. Old orchards have been rooted up. There has been a drift from the land. In 1890 agriculture employed about one-third of the total working population; in 1982 it employed under 6 per cent. Many farmer's sons went off to live in the *Randstad*. Others emigrated. Serious problems of under-employment and an ageing population arose in the farming regions. 'It was a difficult choice for us,' a provincial official told me in Leeuwarden, the capital city of Friesland. 'If more industrial jobs were provided, we might lose our peace, our quietness, our good, clean air. But if we didn't attract more industry, we might have ended up with nothing but old people.' During the Seventies more people went to live in the north. The discovery of the largest natural gasfield in Europe near Groningen has helped to bring more industry, but still not enough, to the north. Delfzijl on the river Eems has been expanded into an industrial port based on natural gas, with the country's first aluminium smelter among the modern plants. Further down river a new industrial port has been built at Eemshaven.

The problems are of a different kind in the southern province of Limburg though they are directly connected with the developments in the north. With the discovery of such large deposits of natural gas in 1960, and the possibility of buying cheaper coal from Poland, Australia and the United States, it was decided to stop

coal-mining in the Netherlands altogether. Coal had only been mined on any large scale since 1902, when the State set up an enterprise, DSM, to open up four pits in the Heerlen area of Limburg. By 1975, in spite of the oil crisis, all the coal mines had been closed and there are no plans to reopen them as the seams are too thin.

Their closure could have brought industrial decay, if not death, to Limburg. But in the 1950s, DSM had decided to expand its chemicals and plastics operations, which it had started twenty years earlier with the production of fertilisers. Natural gas, in which DSM has a 40 per cent share, is piped in from the north; chemical and product pipelines connect their plants with Rotterdam and the Ruhr. Just as the polders give the impression of living at the creation of the world, so, in Limburg, one seems to be living at some turning point in man's constant endeavours to create a new life for himself. The huge surface shafts, sheds, and covered galleries of the mines stand empty, unused now except for the storage of chemical products.

At Beek and Geleen, a few miles away, there is a different form of industrial life. Acres of ground are covered with piping and tubes of different shapes and colours, dominated by tall chimneys, distillation columns and towers. As in a coal mine, the main production process remains concealed from the visitor's sight. Only the result can be observed: millions of little coloured plastic balls streaming down from loading hoppers into plastic bags hour after hour, night and day.

The transformation of the region has been handled with characteristic Dutch care and attention to detail. It has not been easy to cope with the loss of all jobs in the region's major industry in a space of fifteen years. Some older miners have been prematurely retired on pension. Younger men have been retrained, exchanging their chipped, coal-grimed helmets for the new white helmets of the chemical worker. Others have been provided with jobs in new factories which have been attracted to the area, including a Daf car plant. Some have been found new jobs in other parts of the country by the DSM personnel department, which reversed its normal role of finding people for jobs to finding jobs for people. In spite of all these efforts, structural unemployment still remains something of a problem in Limburg. Recently a government

49

agency has been set up to attract new industry, particularly in the high technology area, to the region.

About one-third of all Dutch workers, the same proportion

as in the United States, are employed in industry. What kind of life does the average factory worker lead? Like many other Dutch workers, Piet lives in a post-war block of flats, which has a storage space underneath for his own, his wife's and his two children's bicycles. There is also an open space where he can tinker with his car. (By 1975 there were more cars proportionately in the Netherlands than in Britain).

Piet starts the day with a typically large Dutch breakfast, consisting of a choice of white or brown bread, pumpernickel or honeycake, with slices of ham or cheese, cut into wafer-thin slices, an egg sometimes, margarine instead of butter, jam, and tea or coffee. He goes to work on his bicycle, as he does not live too far away from his place of work. His factory is a modern, brick building with glass-enclosed bridgewalks leading from one section to another and with lawns and trees surrounding it. Like 40 per cent of all workers, Piet belongs to a union which is affiliated to one of the two main federations. Piet was out on strike for a week or so in 1977 over compensation for the rise in the cost-of-living, but that was exceptional. The last time he was on strike before that was in 1960. (The Dutch have far fewer strikes than most other countries. In 1980, only 22,000 man-hours were lost through industrial disputes.) Piet works a 40-hour week, five days a week, about the same number of hours as office workers. In 1981, his income, including holiday bonus and family allowances, was about £8,300 (nearly 15,000 dollars) a year, which was around the national average. In the same year, the minimum wage for both men and women over the age of twenty-three was about £5,000 (9,000 dollars) a year. Nearly a quarter of his wages is deducted for social security payments, which provide him with one of the most generous welfare systems in the world. If Piet loses his job, he receives 75 to 80 per cent of his wages for two-and-a-half years, before he comes on to basic social security, which is still very generous. If Piet is ill he knows that he will receive 80 per cent of his wages from the State for a whole year, though in practice, the

50

employer usually makes up the other 20 per cent. After that, if he is permanently unfit for work, he gets up to 80 per cent of his wages, up to a maximum of £20,000 (36,000 dollars) a year, until he retires.

His whole family is protected by the National Sick Fund, which covers about 80 per cent of the population. This health service provides a full range of free medical treatment and care, or for a small fee. Richer people have to pay or to insure themselves.

Piet knows that when he retires at the age of sixty-five (though some workers quit their job a few years earlier) he will receive a basic State pension which amounted to £4,300 (7,740 dollars) a year for a married couple in 1982; but he is also a member of an occupational pension scheme, which is now compulsory in most industries. As a consequence his total pension will be from 60 to 70 per cent of his average earnings in his last three working years.

Although there is a cafeteria in his factory, Piet takes sandwiches to work just as many of the office workers and executives do. Apart from the farming community, the Dutch rarely eat a large cooked lunch. When Piet is at home he usually has an open sandwich of meat, fish, cheese or sausage, sometimes topped by a fried egg, what the Dutch call an *uitsmijter,* preceded in the winter by a cup of soup. With it, he drinks a glass of milk, of which the Dutch are still quite fond, or a glass of beer. His main meal comes in the evening between six and seven. Soup, which is home-made and delicious, is followed by a meat or fish course of some kind, served with two or more vegetables. At one time, there would have been mounds of potatoes, but with increasing prosperity the Dutch have been eating far more meat, fruit and green vegetables. (They still flavour their mashed potatoes with nutmeg, which they originally brought back to Europe from the Moluccas.) For dessert, there may be *vla* a kind of flavoured custard which his wife buys ready for serving from the milkman who calls at the door, or stewed fruit or a piece of tart. Sometimes he has a glass of beer with his meal and he often has a cigar after it.

After dinner Piet likes to settle down at home with his family and relax. He reads the newspaper thoroughly. Dutch men and women spend on average three-quarters of an hour a day on their paper. He then reads a book or watches television, while his daughter does her homework on the table. Sometimes they have friends in for tea, coffee and cakes, or beer at 8 or 8.30 in the evening. On other nights he goes out to have a drink with his friends in a local bar or café. Occasionally he takes the family to the cinema, but they go there less often than they once did. He doesn't drink much, though his son, who has just started working, goes out drinking in the evening more than Piet ever did when he was a young man. (The consumption of beer increased by 10 per cent between 1975 and 1981, while wine consumption rose even higher by 27 per cent during the same period.) Piet doesn't gamble much either, though he does buy a share in a State lottery ticket or a football pool at work. He hasn't won anything yet, but he's still hoping!

He is careful with his money, but not mean. If he and his wife really want something – a new washing machine, a new television, a new dining room table, they save up for it: hire purchase and credit buying account for only 6 per cent of all consumer spending, one of the lowest proportions in the industrialised world.

One of the real passions and pleasures of Piet's life is football. He played goalkeeper for his local team when he was a young man. Now, every week during the season, he takes along the club's colours to wave and cheer on his team. Piet was a fine skater, too, when he was young and once took part in the arduous Eleven-Towns race in Friesland and actually finished the course, which is no mean feat. He still feels quite excited when the canals freeze over in the winter and, like almost every other Dutch man, woman and child, gets out his skates for a trip across a polder or around the town on ice. At the week-ends or on summer evenings, Piet likes to go to his little allotment, some distance from his home, where he grows vegetables for the kitchen and flowers for the sitting room. He is very fond of his allotment, which he tends with such care that there is never a weed in sight, and he has made the roomy shed into a second home by putting up curtains at the window and installing bunks and a stove. Some of the newer allotment 'sheds' are like miniature houses, with solar heating for the rooms and the glasshouse.

In summer, the whole family goes off by car to France, southern Germany, Spain or Austria in search of the sun and the picturesque. They stay in a modest hotel, pension or apartment, like almost half of the Dutch who go abroad for their holiday, though a third prefer to take their caravan or tent with them. Before they had a car, they used to fly out to one of these countries on a package tour. Piet gets at least three weeks' holiday a year and a holiday bonus which amounts to 7½ per cent of his annual wages.

Is Piet happy with his lot? Like other workers in the western world, he has suffered during the recession. Although inflation has been kept at a respectable level, only 6.7 per cent in 1981, wage increases have been controlled by the government since 1980, so that Piet's real disposable income has fallen slightly in the last two years. But he has the compensation of knowing that some of the money he has lost has been used to create new jobs in the industrial sector in which he is employed and that top salary earners have seen their incomes decline ever more than his. They order things differently in the Netherlands than they do in some other European countries. As the author of a special survey on the country wrote in the influential London weekly, the *Economist,* in January, 1982: 'If somewhere must be found to sit out the recession, Holland must be the nicest, comfiest place to choose.' Piet knows that his wages are still about as high as those in almost any other European country, and much better than in some. And if he is unlucky enough to be made redundant, so that he joins the other 11 per cent of the working population on the dole in the middle of 1982, he has one of the most generous and comprehensive social security systems to look after him and his family.

Since the end of the war there has been a great redistribution

of wealth in the Netherlands. Income tax starts at a modest rate of 17 per cent and rises progressively to 72 per cent on the highest incomes. There is also a wealth tax. In the Civil Service there is already an established ratio of about one to 3½ in net incomes which also applies in most of the private sector, against an after-tax differential in Britain of one to seven.

Some of the Dutch are still rich but none is ostentatious. As a consequence the contrasts in living styles between the different social classes are much less marked than in most other European countries. People of all classes ride bicycles. They all eat more or less the same kind of meals. Many of the middle classes live in rented homes, like a Dutch educationist I once knew, who lived in

53

a small converted farmhouse on the outskirts of the *Randstad*. With its long, twisting corridors and mezzanine floor, it was certainly a far more interesting place to me than a system-built flat or a post-war home, and somewhat more spacious, but it was no better furnished than the homes of many Dutch workers that I have seen.

Outside the *Randstad,* where there is more space, there are some fine, modern luxury homes, built among little orchards at the foot of wooded hills; but in the *Randstad* itself, space and privacy are far more difficult to obtain. You need to be really rich to obtain total privacy. One man I know lives in a small wooded estate. His house is substantially built and comfortably furnished and contains his collections of old masters, antique tulip vases and old china. In the grounds, there is an ultra-modern bungalow where he keeps his Picassos and other works of modern art. Although he is extremely wealthy by Dutch standards, he would not look rich in comparison with some of the surviving landed aristocrats of England, though many of them are now beginning to feel the pinch.

The Dutch have always been modest with their wealth. Their religious principles, the shortage of land, and the absence of a court life during the Dutch republic helped to create the tradition. Money was invested in paintings, furniture and bonds rather than in real estate.

There are of course some differences in the life styles of the various social classes, though much less than in England. (English middle-rank executives are often surprised to be taken out for a business lunch and a glass of beer in a modest restaurant instead of a luxury hotel, not realising that for their Dutch hosts any cooked lunch is luxury compared with their usual sandwiches!) The middle classes eat more or less the same kind of food as the workers do, though they are more likely to have a glass of sherry or a Dutch gin before their meal at home, and one or two glasses of wine with it, on special occasions at least. The upper middle classes often have some help in the home – a cleaning lady who comes in once or twice a week. They also spend more than other classes on outside entertainment – concerts, ballet, opera, the theatre and visits to restaurants on anniversaries and special occasions. Young people eat out far more than their elders,

J. DALENOORD

favouring trendy, candle-lit *bistros* and pizza houses.

Compared to the English, the Dutch tend to dine early, and some of the more traditional restaurants close by 10 p.m., even in the biggest cities, though newer restaurants are open to much later hours, while clubs stay open all night. Like the English, the Dutch have gained a great gastronomic legacy from their former overseas territories and in almost every town there are restaurants, serving Indonesian and/or Chinese food. They are decorated in the native style and the waiters, in the more expensive places at least, wear native costume. At the end of the night, it is not uncommon to see the manageress or owner totalling up the takings on an abacus, as speedily and accurately as on a modern electronic calculator.

These restaurants serve many delicious, exotic dishes, including that gourmet meal for gluttons, *rijsttafel* (literally, rice table). This superlative meal consists of a dozen or more different spiced meat, fish and vegetable dishes, a bowl of rice and a bowl of soup. Old hands from the tropics maintain the traditional way of eating the meal, never mixing the side dishes in with the rice. And then, as you might expect, there are the fish restaurants, serving really excellent dishes, though some of the best are hidden away, as if the Dutch wanted to keep them to themselves! One of the best is in the northern part of The Hague, with waiters who all wear long white aprons and speak excellent English, marble-topped tables and a comfortable bar for an aperitif. Before the meal, they give you a free fish snack as an appetiser and after it, as a final imaginative touch, a chocolate in the shape of a fish. So who said the Dutch were mean! In the last couple of years there has been a phenomenal increase in the number and variety of foreign restaurants in the big cities, so that there is not only a wide choice of French and Italian restaurants, but also Indian, Greek and Argentinian and many more.

Many middle-class people have a second holiday: boating in the north, skiing in Austria or Switzerland, or visiting London, Paris or Rome in the off-season. A smaller proportion have a second home – a chalet-style bungalow or a converted farmhouse or a cottage. An even smaller number have a second home abroad, some of them in isolated villages in Ireland or Italy, but most in France or Spain. Foreign visitors often find it difficult to identify the different social classes, though it is much easier for the Dutch to do so; but there are other divisions in society which were, until recently, of far greater importance to them.

The 'pillars of society' has a different meaning in the Nether-

lands from what it does elsewhere. Religion has always been one of the dominant forces in society. It was one of the main causes, but not the only one, of the Dutch revolt against Spanish rule in the sixteenth century. But the Dutch were never – before, during or even after the war of independence – entirely Protestant. There

J. Dalenoord.

Lange Voorhout, den Haag

was always a large Catholic minority, which was officially proscribed, but which was treated with tolerance in most of the provinces and allowed to worship in its own way in private as the chapel of Our Lord in the Attic in Amsterdam still testifies. By the end of the eighteenth century it was estimated that one-third of the population was Catholic. The Catholic hierarchy was re-established in 1853.

By the last quarter of the nineteenth century, when the modern political parties started to be formed, the country was firmly divided on religious lines. The Catholics' main strength lay in the two southern provinces of Limburg and North Brabant. The Protestants were particularly strong north of the big rivers and in the islands of Zeeland. But the Protestants were not so united as the Catholics. By then, they had split into the present two main churches, the Dutch Reformed and the smaller, more doctrinaire, Reformed church, which believes that the Calvinist confession should be interpreted literally and should be strictly applied in daily life.

There were, and still are, many other smaller breakaway sects, including Christian Reformed, Old Reformed, Remonstrant, Free Evangelist, the Netherlands Protestant Union and others. Some of these smaller sects have strange-sounding convictions for modern times, like being opposed to all forms of inoculation and insurance. In addition to these religious groups, there were other people who believed that the country should be organised on 'neutral' or non-denominational lines. These included both socialists and liberals.

The Dutch are an earnest and committed people, with a fundamentalist tendency to believe implicitly in the correctness of their own views. Each *bloc* was fighting for its emancipation; the political parties which were formed reflected these views. The first political party of modern times, the Anti-revolutionary party, was started in 1878 by the more doctrinaire Protestants to combat the secularising effects of the French revolution. Other parties followed: Liberal, Socialist, Catholic, and another Protestant party, the Christian Historical Union. There were also many splinter parties, both denominational and 'neutral'.

All of them were much more than political parties in the normal sense. They were fighting not just for political power alone, but for deep convictions or religious principles, a total and committed way of life. The party leaders sought to isolate and to contain their supporters in separate organisations; as a reward, the leaders tried to provide their supporters with institutions of their own. The three main groups – Catholic, Protestant and 'neutral' – formed the pillars of society.

It was not only political parties which were organised along these lines, but practically the whole of society, including trade unions and schools. A boy, or girl, could be educated in institutions of his own religious faith from the age of four to twenty-five, first in a kindergarten run by members of his church, then at a denominational school, and finally at the Protestant Free University of Amsterdam or at the Catholic University of Nijmegen. People could read newspapers coloured by their own views and borrow books from Catholic, Protestant or 'neutral' libraries. When broadcasting started in the 1920s, the Dutch could listen to Catholic, Protestant, Socialist and 'neutral' radio stations, just as they can still watch television programmes provided by the same organisations today. If they were ill, they could be nursed back to health by the 'neutral' Green Cross, the Catholic White-Yellow Cross or the Protestant Orange-Green Cross organisations. They could play in Catholic or Protestant football leagues, or join women's organisations, where they would be sure to meet people of their own faith or of none.

The associations became so numerous that the Catholics needed a book of a thousand pages to list all of them. There was even a Catholic goat breeders' association and Catholic, Protestant and 'neutral' pigeon clubs! People lived in self-contained communities and tended to have friends of their own faith, to buy goods from shopkeepers of the same religious persuasion, to work in firms where all the employees had the same religion. The Dutch call this process *verzuiling,* or pillarisation. For fifty years or more, it succeeded in maintaining a stable, if sometimes wasteful, divided and rather inward-looking society. But it made people exaggerate their divisions and their differences. Even as late as 1954 it was possible for the Catholic bishops to issue a pastoral letter prohibiting Catholics from joining a Socialist union or listening to Socialist broadcasts, an action which would be unthinkable in the Netherlands nowadays.

Under the pressure of modern industrialised life many of the pillars have started to crumble. The divisions don't mean nearly as much to most of the young generation as they did to some older people. Intermarriage between men and women of different religious faiths, which was unusual at one time particularly in the more remote provinces, is now commonplace. The need for mobility, created by modern industry, has made Catholics take jobs in the north and Protestants in the south, helping to erode the old north-south divisions. Universities have been freed with Catholic students and lecturers at the Free University of Amsterdam

J. BALENDORD

Staphorst

and Protestant students and professors at Catholic Nijmegen. But the system of providing three different schools – Protestant, Catholic and 'neutral' – still persists even in the new polder villages. These schools are all subsidised by the State, as is guaranteed by law, so that parents can have the kind of education for their children that they want. But even in schools, where pillarisation was most entrenched, there are some signs of change. The first school for all three groups has been opened at Zoetermeer near The Hague. And in the predominantly Catholic south, some Catholics, who have come from other parts of the country, send their children to Protestant schools, because they are less crowded and their children can receive more intensive attention.

What has helped to lessen the divisions in society is the changing balance of religious faiths. In 1960, the Catholics became the largest religious group in the Netherlands for the first time, having more adherents than all the Protestant churches combined. This tendency has continued, so that the Catholics are no longer a minority fighting as they did before the last war for full emancipation in public appointments and commercial jobs. At the same time, some of the smaller Protestant sects have started to shake off their more rigid beliefs. When there was an epidemic of polio some ten years ago in Staphorst, one of the strictest Protestant villages, most parents defied their pastor's advice and had their children inoculated.

But the main reason for the crumbling of the pillars has been the rapid growth in the number of people who belong to no church, the 'unchurchly' as the Dutch still call them, who now account for 25 to 30 per cent of the population. This growing disenchantment has forced the churches to come closer to each other in the ecumenical movement where they can bear joint witness to their faith. But is has not been easy for all church leaders to subscribe to these changes and some still hanker after their past authority and power. 'Pillarisation has been replaced by polarisation,' Professor Dr. H. A. M. Fiolet, secretary of the Dutch Council of Churches, told me during a conversation in the book-lined study of his home near Utrecht. 'There is no longer a vertical division in society, but a horizontal split.' As in other European countries, the main conflict has been resolved into that between the conservative forces in society and the supporters of a more open and progressive way of life, though in the Netherlands this is still tempered by their individual history.

These changes are most evident in parliament, where

150 members of the lower house are elected for a four-year term under a system of proportional representation. In the last few general elections, there has been a gradual decline in support for religious-based parties and an increase in the number of floating voters. As a consequence, the three main religious parties have presented a united front since 1977 as the Christian Democrat Alliance, a merger of the former Catholic People's Party and the Protestant Anti-Revolutionary Party and the Christian Historical Union. In the 1981 elections, the Christian Democrat Alliance was the biggest party with 48 seats, but the Labour Party's share was cut from 53 to 44 and the right-wing Liberal Party's from 28 to 26. Democrats '66, which like the recently-formed Social Democratic Party in Britain, is opposed to dogmatic views of both the left and the right, more than doubled its representation from 8 to 17. But the Dutch still like to express their individual viewpoints, so that in the last few decades, there has always been half-a-dozen smaller parties with one to three seats. In the 1981 elections, six other parties also gained a handful of seats – three extreme Protestant parties, the Radicals, the Communists and the Pacifist-Socialists.

Since the end of the war no party has ever gained enough seats to form a government by itself. This could have produced a highly unstable situation, but for one other major characteristic of the Dutch. Although they are people of causes and convictions, they are also realists and prepared eventually to compromise.

Verzuiling produced rigid divisions at the bottom of the society; but toleration produced coalitions at the top. After every election it often takes many weeks and sometimes months for the party leaders to form a new coalition government. In 1972, it took a record time of nearly six months. But once a coalition has been formed, it tends to be fairly stable and to remain in office for its full term of four years. But the coalition government formed in 1981 of the Christian Democrat Alliance, the Labour Party and Democrats '66, did not last that long. It foundered over a Labour

61

Party plan to spend nearly £1,000 million (1,800 million dollars) to create new jobs. New elections were held in September, 1982 when the biggest gains were made by the right-wing Liberals. In November, a coalition government of Liberals and Christian Democrats came to power.

The Dutch have one of the most complex and subtle systems of government in the world, combining some of the best features of other democratic systems. As in the United States, ministers are not members of parliament, or even necessarily ex-members, though as ministers they may speak in either house and regularly do so. A minister, however, has no other rôle in parliament. But, as in Britain, parliament is sovereign and has the final right to vote a government out of office, which has happened on several occasions in the post-war years, and also to reject or to amend any Bill. Under this dualistic system, the government is expected to govern, which it does with a mixture of paternalism and technocratic and managerial skills. It is not unknown for a minister to bring a blackboard into parliament to elucidate points for deputies: the Dutch take a great delight in organisational charts, complicated plans and comprehensive diagrams. Members of parliament represent basically the pure clear voice of uncompromising principle. It is common for deputies to vote against the government, even though it contains members of their own party. This may seem an unwieldy way of running a country, but the Dutch can do this daily, multiple balancing act with uncommon skill.

A similar system is used with equal effectiveness in the municipal councils. The government-appointed, salaried burgomaster and the aldermen, who are elected by the council from its own members take the place of the government while the members of the council act as a parliament.

Government can be strong and stable; minority voices can be heard in the corridors of power. The system gets the best of both worlds, something for which the Dutch seem to have a special facility.

The stability of society has its roots deep in Dutch history. In the nineteenth century, the government succeeded in gaining full ministerial responsibility from the king twenty years before parliament learnt to exercise its power. Industry developed late so

that the bourgeoisie was firmly entrenched long before an industrial proletariat had appeared, except in a few cities such as Amsterdam. Even earlier than that, the ruling regents and merchants of the cities had created a stable, middle-of-the-road society which was in many ways highly civilised, humanitarian and tolerant.

From the seventeenth century the Dutch have always opened their doors wide to foreign refugees, such as the Jews or the Huguenots. The tradition continues to this day. In the post-war years foreigners from many parts of the world have found asylum in the Netherlands, including White Russians, Chileans, Ugandan Asians, Kurds and Americans who were opposed to the Vietnam war. Many groups have been provided with free headquarters in the exclusive banking and insurance area in the capital, with jobs and accommodation.

In the late 1960s and the early 1970s, when Amsterdam became a magnet for 'freaks' and 'drop-outs' from all over the world, the city's authorities showed a remarkable tolerance to these new kinds of visitors. The Vondel park was given over to these 'guests' as a free sleeping place. The city spent hundreds of thousands of guilders in providing washing, toilet and other facilities, but complaints by Dutch neighbours about night-time noise and day-time litter forced the city to close the park to 'hippies' after a three-year-long experiment.

'Ah, but those are foreigners,' a young girl student told me in Utrecht. 'The Dutch aren't nearly so tolerant to each other as they are to people from abroad.' There may have been some truth in this remark in the past, but it is much less valid today. Dutch rebels and progressives are not persecuted by the establishment. They are far more often brought inside and encouraged to taste the realities of responsibility and power. The mass media, the church and education have all been infiltrated by progressives. For this reason change is probably more often implemented from the inside than from the outside in the Netherlands. Society is basically stable and the Dutch, therefore, are not afraid to experiment. In the 1960s, the Provo movement gained global publicity for its progressive plans. It wanted to provide free city transport in Amsterdam by using white-painted bicycles and to cut down on air pollution by providing a fleet of computer-

controlled electric cars. Although some 'white' bicycles and, later, a number of 'white' cars appeared on the streets, the campaign did not have much success.

But nobody has forgotten the following period of the Gnomes, or *Kabouters*. In the early 1970s a new protest group of *Kabouters* declared itself independent of the authorities and set up its own alternative ministries, including a Ministry of Housing to occupy and improve derelict houses, and a Ministry of Social Affairs to organise help for old people. The Amsterdammers were willing to give the *Kabouters* a chance and elected five members to the city

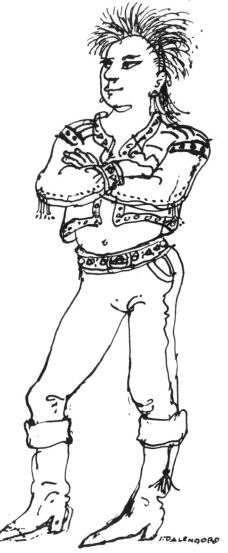

council. But the *Kabouters* didn't have much of an impact, and that movement has also withered away. They have been succeeded by the *Krakers,* or squatters, who rioted as a protest against homelessness during the inauguration of Queen Beatrix in April, 1980. Since then, they have had several violent confrontations with the police. There are now about 10,000 squatters in Amsterdam and more in other big cities. Like all groups in the Netherlands, the squatters are highly organised. They even had their own pirate radio station and walkie-talkie sets to call up reinforcements whenever the police arrived to make an eviction. Although older Dutch people have some sympathy for the squatters' plight, many have been disturbed by the ferocity of their battles with the police. But not all protests in the Netherlands end in violence. It still remains uncharacteristic. For example, the peace march held in Amsterdam on November 21, 1981, passed off without incident, even though it attracted 400,000 demonstrators. It was four times bigger than any other demonstration in Dutch post-war history and the biggest march for peace ever held in Europe.

Obviously, Dutch society, like any other, has its faults.

To some of the Dutch it can seem stifling, mediocre, second-rate. But then the Dutch are their own sternest critics. They are contemptuous of idle praise and suspicious of flattery. They don't like to hide their defects. When one foreign ruler was on a State visit to the Netherlands, his official tour took him past the canal barges where some people live in the overcrowded capital. The previous monarch, Queen Juliana, would break off tours of new housing estates to chat with housewives about the difficulties of life and of bringing up a family in the modern age. She had a right to do so, as she has some experience of ordinary life. Like any other Dutch housewife, she rides a bicycle, buys some of her clothes ready-made in local stores, and sent her four daughters to the primary school just down the road. Queen Juliana would sometimes drive down to collect them – and give a lift to any other children who were going her way. The present monarch, Queen Beatrix, also sends her three sons to ordinary schools and, so I am told, still sees some of her former fellow-students from Leiden University, not only because she likes them, but also because their less fettered experience helps her to keep in touch with normal life.

It is this open, unpretentious quality of life which appeals to me most in the Netherlands. Recently, a mobile coffee stall and seats for tourists and pedestrians have been thoughtfully provided right in the middle of the central square of the Houses of Parliament in the Hague. Obviously, this lack of pretension is not total, but a man – or a woman – is expected to live up to his position; he is only looked down on when he pretends to be something he is not. There is a simple courtesy, a genuine curiosity, and a rugged independence, which seem to be disappearing fast in many other western countries.

There have to be rules, particularly in such a crowded country, where there is not much elbow room. But they are not inflexible; if necessary, they can be bent. The Dutch know how to improvise and to deal with emergencies. They do things with a quiet kind of relaxed efficiency, which is very different in its cause and effect from that to be found in some other countries noted for efficiency. There is not merely a mechanistic application of rules, but a logical attention to detail.

In the last few years there has been an economic miracle

in the Netherlands. The first industrial revolution, based on coal, iron and steel, lasted only a generation or so, and the Dutch went almost straight from a mercantilist empire refusing to invest in heavy industries at home into modern, second-stage industrial economy. Even before the last war, firm foundations for the change had been laid. The Netherlands was one of the first nations to develop modern multinational companies operating in the growth sectors of petroleum, electronics, food processing and chemicals. Despite the world-wide recession, the Dutch still have a lot going for them economically. At the beginning of the Sixties, the discovery of huge reserves of natural gas in Groningen helped to heat their homes, to fuel the profitable sectors of oil-refining, chemicals and steel, to provide a valuable, and truly invisible, export, and to subsidise their generous social security system. But the oil crisis of the Seventies and the recession of the Eighties have forced the Dutch to trim their sails. Gas prices followed the rise in oil prices, threatening to blow the guilder sky-high, which, in alliance with high unit wage costs in industry, would have made their exports uncompetitive. Accordingly, by the end of the Seventies the government had decided to reduce gas output and to fill the energy gap by importing cheap coal for use in power stations, and to turn some of it into synthetic gas in new gasification plants, two of which are already planned for Rotterdam and Eemshaven. At the same time, public spending has been trimmed back to cut the budget deficit and a successful incomes policy has helped to reduce unit wage costs dramatically in the last couple of years. But these measures have failed to cure all the economic problems which have affected even the industrial giants like Royal Dutch/Shell, heavily committed to oil and petrochemicals, and Philips, which has had to face severe competition from the Japanese in consumer electronics. But these multinationals are big and wealthy enough to consolidate and fight for themselves. In the last few years, much government aid to industry has been channelled into the new growth areas of aerospace, microelectronics and biotechnology, where the Dutch already have quite a number of thriving companies. The Fokker aircraft company, which produced the best-selling Friendship and Fellowship planes, plans to make a bigger 150-seater aircraft in alliance with an American firm. Philips remains one of the world leaders in electronics. And

Roosenburg

the Dutch firm of Gist-Brocades, one of the leaders in pharmaceuticals and enzymes, and the Anglo-Dutch multinational, Unilever, are experimenting on the margins of the new field of biotechnology, particularly in the food industry.

Food processing still plays an important part in the Dutch economy with huge exports of such goods as cheese, condensed milk, canned meat and tinned beer. The diamond industry has been built up again, after the deportation of thousands of Jewish workers during the Second World War, and the Amsterdam cut is still a hallmark of craftsmanship among diamond dealers throughout the world. International trade in ready-to-wear clothing has been boosted by the building of a brand-new *Confectiecentrum* near Schiphol airport, which contains the showrooms and sales offices of more than two hundred Dutch manufacturers and sales agents.

The Dutch have retained their traditional role as the 'carriers of Europe' no longer only by sea but also now by land and air. Rotterdam-Europoort, the largest port in the world, is the main gateway to the European Economic Community. The inland port of Amsterdam has been modernised and expanded and linked to the hinterland of Europe by a renewed Amsterdam-Rhine canal, which is lit at night to make it safer, while greatly extended port facilities in Delfzijl in the far north-east and in Flushing in the south-west, which is strategically situated for trade with England, Belgium and northern France, are now being built up and developed.

Huge trucks from many different countries thunder along the motorways: more than half of all the international road haulage in the Community begins or ends in the Netherlands. Almost half of the goods transported along the canals and waterways are carried in foreign barges: German barges taking a short cut across the Netherlands to northern Germany and Belgian barges taking goods from Antwerp to the Rhine. Schiphol airport, about seven miles from Amsterdam, was rebuilt in 1967 to handle the biggest jumbo jets and is one of the busiest airports in the European Community, handling nearly 10 million passengers a year.

The tourist industry has expanded greatly and in the last few years the Netherlands has begun to develop as an international conference centre by building ultra-modern congress buildings in

The Hague, Amsterdam, and Utrecht. Banking, insurance and dealing in stocks and shares remains an important aspect of the economic life of Amsterdam, whose stock exchange quotes more American securities than any other exchange in Europe. Youngish men, trendily dressed in heavy black sweaters and jeans, sit in cafés over a cup of coffee playing the international markets in the *Wall Street Journal* as confidently as their ancestors dealt in foreign government bonds, while their more soberly dressed contemporaries in insurance and banker's offices send telexes around the world with as much dexterity as their predecessors despatched sailing ships out to the Orient to bring back precious cargoes of spices.

The transition to a modern industrial state had been made with a minimum of friction. Regular talks between trade unions and employers were started long before the Second World War. In 1950 a Social-Economic Council, composed of an equal number of representatives of the government, employers and unions, was set up to advise the government on social and economic questions, a task it has done with a considerable amount of success. In the same year, works councils were also established in large firms, and their powers have gradually been expanded, particularly since 1979 when a new law came into force. Under this Act, an employer is forced to present the company's annual accounts to the works council every year, whether they have to be published elsewhere or not. He also has to obtain the works council's consent in a wide range of matters, including pensions, profit-sharing, working-time, merit systems and holidays. Moreover, a member of a works council cannot be dismissed, except for serious misconduct or if the business, or his division of the company, is closed. There is much less resentment about these stringent controls over the independence of employers than there would be in many other countries. 'If we have a problem,' an official in the Ministry of Economic Affairs told me, 'we like to discuss it with everyone involved. You never know who's going to come up with the right solution.'

The Dutch really do believe in talks and consultations. Whenever they have one of their rare strikes, they worry just as much over the reason why the talking failed, as they do over the lost production, which is usually minimal by international standards. When the

Municipal Council's plan for the redevelopment of the old Jordaan district in Amsterdam provoked a storm of protest in 1969, the council sent out questionnaires to all eight thousand inhabitants of the district, asking for their views. Only two hundred or so questionnaires were ever filled in and returned to the town hall. 'Apparently, Jordaan inhabitants do not like questionnaires,' the city authorities said blandly and sympathetically. And to prove that they were not involved in a mere publicity exercise, they commissioned a market research organisation to find out what the residents really did want. Obviously, in a highly complex industrial society, not every single individual viewpoint can be catered for; but no one can blame the

River Yssel, Dieren

Dutch authorities for not trying.

Industrialisation, however, has brought penalties as well as privileges. Despite efforts at international control, the Rhine has become a multinational sewer full of chemical wastes and sewage. Unfortunately for the Dutch, they are on the receiving end. It is no longer possible as it was in 1874 to set up a plant in Rotterdam to take fresh, clean water from the Rhine. Neither is it possible to meet the ever-increasing demands for water from the crowded *Randstad* by draining it from the sand dunes along the coast which act as a natural purifying plant for rainwater. If too much water is taken out, the dunes become too dry and the salt water, which is only a few feet below the surface, rises, polluting

drinking supplies and making the adjacent land too salt to grow crops.

The control of water supplies is much less apparent than the creation of new lands from the seabed, but it is no less complex or important. Water, which is already partially purified, is piped from the Rhine to the sand dunes so that more drinking water can be made available for the crowded cities.

The Zuyder Zee works made Lake IJssel the country's biggest fresh water reservoir. But in dry weather, such as the summer of 1976, the level of the lake falls. So a moveable weir has been built west of Arnhem to divert more of the waters of the Rhine up the river IJssel and into the lake. Water is pumped out of the lake every night to flush out the canals of the capital. The dirty water is eventually discharged through the North Sea Canal which connects Amsterdam with the sea. The dams in the Delta project divert more water from the Rhine into the fresh water lakes which have been formed between the islands of Zeeland.

The Dutch have been one of the leading nations in the fight against pollution. Since 1970 the government has accepted the principle that the polluter must pay, though this is difficult to enforce without much greater international co-operation. A nation-wide chain of three hundred, computer-controlled monitoring stations has been built to sniff out sulphur dioxide in the air. Permission to build a new steelworks at Rotterdam was recently refused, unless the company could show that pollution would be kept within very stringent limits.

Some big Dutch companies think the best idea might be to shift all the pollution-prone industries out of the country altogether and put them on a man-made island out at sea. In 1975, thirty companies spent £ 500,000 (850,000 dollars) on investigating a scheme to create an artificial island some twelve miles or more off the coast by diking a part of the North Sea and making an off-shore polder. The island would be used for oil refineries, nuclear plants and storage plants for liquid gas which will be shipped in from North Africa when Dutch natural gas starts to run out towards the end of the century. The government was also very interested in the plan and set up its own committee to investigate it.

This bold scheme raises many problems: legal, financial, social,

72

technical. 'We would have to decide,' a Ministry of Transport official told me, 'whether the ten thousand workers would live on the island or whether they would commute there every day by helicopter. That's just one of the many problems involved. But we like to be prepared so that if anyone ever does want an industrial island out at sea, we've done our homework, and we can go ahead with building it straight away.'

But industrialisation has also brought its privileges. It

has made it possible for the Dutch to spend more on some of their cherished projects. They have long had a great concern for the poor, the old and the sick. As Cornelius Cayley, an eighteenth-century visitor, noted: 'One thing the Dutch are much to be commended for, that is, their care of the poor ... After the gates of their towns are shut in the evening, whoever they are opened to, pay something, which is applied to the poor.' The money went to support *hofjes,* those delightful little groups of almshouses in quiet closes which can still be seen in many Dutch towns to this day. They still accommodate about four thousand old people, and most of the picturesque homes are so popular that there is a long waiting list.

In modern times, the greatest achievements have been made in the care of the mentally sick and the physically handicapped. The Dutch pioneered the use of sheltered workshops of which they have nearly two hundred in many different parts of the country. The handicapped and the mentally ill can work at their own jobs at their own pace and receive up to 95 per cent of normal, outside wages for doing so. There are a number of half-way homes, supervised by a psychiatrist, in which mental hospital patients can learn to readapt to the outside world. Some patients are boarded out in private homes, while others from the van der Hoeven clinic in Utrecht make regular visits to private homes in the city. There are some purpose-built hotels for the physically handicapped and the Dutch Red Cross has a hospital ship, the *Henri Dunant,* which provides hundreds of the permanently disabled with a holiday cruise every year.

Near Arnhem there is *Het Dorp,* the Village, where all the residents are severely handicapped people, each living in a

J. DA LE NOORD

73

bed-sitting room with its own bathroom. Most of the residents are in wheelchairs, but they can get around their village quite easily even in the worst weather, as the main street is heated and covered by glass. They are not isolated from the world outside. The residents administer their own village. And some of the four hundred residents work in Arnhem. There are two guest rooms attached to each block of ten dwellings. *Het Dorp* has become an international showpiece and is visited by social workers from dozens of different countries each year. The money to build it – £3,600,000 (6,120,000 dollars) – was raised by a television appeal in about twenty-four hours.

Jean Pesynhofje, Leiden

J. DALENOORD

Another striking innovation has been made in a different sphere – the treatment of criminals. In recent years, Dutch judges have tried the experiment of drastically reducing the length of prison sentences. Because this has been coupled with more intensive care and treatment of offenders, there has been no significant increase in the crime rate by international standards. The last few months of a sentence is usually served in an open prison, which is indistinguishable from the private houses on either side. The prisoners go out every day, without supervision, to do a normal day's work.

Charity begins at home, but the Dutch also extend their concern to the victims of earthquakes, wars and famines in other parts of the world. They put their money where their heart is. Appeals can raise millions of guilders from the Dutch public overnight. The government has one of the best records in the world for financial aid to developing countries, which has reached a record level in the last four or five years. Despite the current economic difficulties, aid amounted to nearly £1,000 million (1,800 million dollars) in 1981, or 1.5 per cent of the net national income, about three times more than that provided on average by other members of the O.E.C.D. As the Minister for Development Cooperation said recently: 'Our own national problems may be serious, but those of some 800 million people in the developing countries are many times worse.' Whatever government is in power, it seems likely that aid will be maintained at this generous level, though some of it may be diverted into spheres which are of more benefit to Dutch exporters. But some Dutch people are beginning to wonder how any nation, even one which is so greatly committed to international aid and social welfare, can continue to sustain such generous expenditure at home and abroad particularly after exports of gas cease in about ten years, when it will be necessary to increase other exports by some 30 per cent just to compensate.

Few other small countries, and even some of the larger ones,

treat their artists as well as the Dutch do. The government fixes some of the salaries, such as those of musicians, and subsidises their pensions. One-and-a-half per cent of the cost of government buildings and 1 per cent of the cost of schools and universities is earmarked for decorative art – murals, sculptures, stained glass. Artists of all kinds – painters, sculptors, weavers, potters – who can't make a living can be commissioned by their town or city council to produce work which is then bought by the council with the aid of a government subsidy and exhibited in schools, hospitals and other public buildings. In this way, they are guaranteed a basic wage, equivalent to social security, and some of them are also provided with a rent-free studio or flat. The authorities also subsidise literary magazines, theatre workshops and other experimental projects.

These policies have produced variable results, but there is little doubt that they have helped to contribute to the artistic and cultural renaissance in the Netherlands in the last few years. Amsterdam has become one of the most stimulating and intellectually vital cities in Europe. It has something of the atmosphere of Paris in the 1930s, with its thousand practising painters and sculptors, its American colony, its crowded bars, its intense discussion, and its serious draughts players crouched over their boards in cafés around the Leidseplein.

Everyone has heard of Rembrandt and van Gogh. In Amsterdam, you can visit the house where Rembrandt lived and worked for twenty years, which is now a museum containing 250 of his etchings, while the best collection of his paintings may be seen in the Rijksmuseum, across a few canals. Nearby, there is a superb modern museum, devoted to the development of van Gogh, which attracts half-a-million visitors a year. The Dutch don't want to forget their artistic past, but neither do they want to be perpetually reminded of it. They are living now. And in the last decade or so, their achievements have begun to make a significant impact on other countries again. Ballet has been officially sponsored for only a few years, but the two main companies, the Dutch National Ballet and the Netherlands Dance Theatre, have already made an international reputation. Opera has an equally short history, but a number of Dutch singers have recently achieved international fame, particularly Gré van Swol-Brouwesteyn, Christine Deutekom and Elly Ameling.

Music has a longer history. There are few families in which someone does not play a musical instrument or sing in a choir.

The Concertgebouw Orchestra of Amsterdam, now under conductor Bernard Haitink, has had a high international reputation for many years. There are nine other symphony orchestras in the country and a number of smaller chamber music groups. Government subsidies have helped to encourage the composition of many new symphonies, electronic works and audio-visual experiments. Among the modern composers whose work is best known abroad are Willem Pijper and Henk Badings. Painting, the traditional art of the Netherlands, has again brought a number of Dutchmen international fame. Among the established artists there are Appel, Corneille and Co Westerik, while younger painters are among the leaders of the latest international trends. The reputations of great artists have always flitted easily over national boundaries, but writers in one of the less common languages find it far more difficult to make their voices heard throughout the world. For this reason, Dutch literature has never gained its proper share of recognition ever since their greatest author, Joost van den Vondel, was writing his plays and poems in the seventeenth century. In the present century, Louis Couperus never received the wide acclaim he deserved for his finely detailed novels of high life in The Hague. The works of Simon Vestdijk, who died in 1971, were translated into many languages, but his international reputation never matched his multitude of talents.

Since the end of the war, there has been something of a resurgence in Dutch literature, but their new writers have found it equally difficult to break through the language barrier. The most impressive contemporary writers are Gerard Kornelis van het Reve, whose first novel, *The Evenings,* created a sensation in the Netherlands when it was published in 1947 and who has been a controversial figure ever since; Harry Mulisch who has recently turned from novels and short stories to reportage on the Eichmann trial and the Provo movement; and Willem Frederik Hermans, formerly attached to the geophysics department of Groningen University, who has written some powerful novels about the Second World War and other subjects. There are many other writers such as Jan Wolkers and Teun de Vries, but none has gained the wider audience they deserve. In the cinema, some prize-winning documentaries have been made by directors such as Bert Haanstra and in the last few years there have been one or two interesting long films and television plays.

And so one could go on. In many spheres the Dutch have started to make a mark again. Professional football did not start in the Netherlands until 1954, but in 1970 Feyenoord of Rotterdam won the European Cup and in the following three seasons it was won by Ajax of Amsterdam. In 1974, the Dutch lost to West Germany by one goal in the final of the World Cup. Recently, Dutch football has temporarily lost some of its shine, but, in compensation, they have had great success in hockey and in March, 1982, the Dutch yachtsman, Cornelis van Rietschoten was the outright winner of the Whitbread round-the-world race.

The Dutch have taken many top prizes in international ice skating events. Hilbert van der Duin became world speed skating champion in 1982 and Dianne de Leeuw became the women's figure skating champion. They have also produced some top cyclists, including Jan Janssen and Joop Zoetemelk who both won the Tour de France. In 1975 Hennie Kuiper won the professional world road race championship while André Gevers became the amateur champion. Wim Ruska won two gold medals for judo in the 1972 Olympic Games. Tom Okker and Betty Stöve are both well-known in the international tennis circuits.

It is not only these achievements which make the Nether-

lands such an interesting place today. There is something else of greater import. The German poet, Heinrich Heine, was reputed to have said that if the world was coming to an end he would go to the Netherlands, where everything happens fifty years later. There may have been some truth in his remark in the nineteenth century, but the opposite is true today. The Netherlands is a better indicator of the future than the past. So very many of the contemporary problems which now afflict industrial nations in other parts of the world have been experienced by the Dutch for many years: a great density of population, pollution, shortage of water supplies and of raw materials, lack of living space. At the same time, many of their solutions to the problems of the modern world have been increasingly adopted elsewhere: consensus politics, multinational companies, physical planning, high taxation for increased social services, cycling for health reasons, and yachting (a Dutch word in origin) as one of the last means of escape into solitude. 'Going dutch' has become fashionable again. The philosophy that activates Dutch society is a simple one. It is a recognition that each individual has to face the responsibilities of living in a community, but that the community should encourage the individual to remain independent nevertheless. The Dutch know that their country is only small. They wouldn't like to exaggerate their virtues and their capabilities any more than they want to hide their defects. But if you've got to have modern, industrialised welfare societies – and no-one yet has come up with a better alternative – then the Dutch model is as good as any in the world or, maybe, even the best. But some of the younger Dutch people are not wholly convinced that they've got it right. They are questioning and examining the basis tenets of modern society as vigorously as any young progressive anywhere. As in so many other aspects of life, you tend to get the best of both worlds in the Netherlands.

St. Servaasbrug, Maastricht

FRANK E. HUGGETT, who was born in London and educated at Wadham College, Oxford, has been a student of the Dutch scene for many years. He is the author of *The Modern Netherlands* (Pall Mall, London; Praeger, New York, 1971) which gives a detailed account of many different aspects of the country – political, religious, cultural, social, educational and economic – and of a companion volume, *Modern Belgium,* 1969. He has also written a general survey, *The Netherlands,* illustrated with many colour plates, and a companion volume to this book, **The Dutch Connection,** which describes the influence that the Dutch have had on the rest of the world. In addition he has written many other books, mainly on British social history, including the best-seller, *Life Below Stairs,* an account of domestic service from Victorian times. A former member of the editorial staff of the *Daily Telegraph,* London, he is now a full-time writer and lecturer who has travelled extensively in Europe. His wife is also a writer and a poet. He has one daughter.

Published by: Ministry of Foreign Affairs, The Hague, Netherlands
Production: Government publishing office, The Hague
All rights reserved
Lay-out: Ton van Riel
Printed by: Government Printing Office, The Hague

ISBN 90 12 04247 X   307828D